Wealth Psychology

Russom Teklay

Wealth Psychology

ISBN: 9798224144280

Dedication

To my family, whose unwavering support gave me the courage to dream across continents, and to every reader seeking freedom through financial self-mastery.

Foreword

A foreword by a financial psychologist or successful entrepreneur could lend credibility and introduce the book's themes.

Acknowledgments

I am deeply grateful to my mentors, editors, and the countless individuals who shared their financial stories with me. Special thanks to my partner and friends, who believed in this project even when I doubted.

About the author

Born in the heart of Eritrea, my life began under the shadow of a military dictatorship, an oppressive regime that I knew I had to escape to seek freedom and fulfill my potential. My journey was one of resilience and determination. I completed my secondary education amidst the challenges of my homeland, a testament to my enduring spirit and quest for knowledge.

In 2014, a pivotal year, I made a life-changing decision to leave Eritrea. My path led me to Germany, a land of opportunity and hope. Here, in 2017, I was granted the chance to start anew when my stay was officially approved. Embracing this new chapter, I immersed myself in learning the German language, a key that unlocked new doors in this foreign land.

My journey of education continued in Germany, where I not only completed my German school leaving certificate but also embarked on a path that resonated with my passion for technology. Hanover became my new home, a city where I found my calling. I delved into the world of information technology, specifically in the healthcare system.

My perseverance and hard work culminated in successfully completing further training, leading me to become an IT system administrator in the healthcare sector, specializing in Digital Health System Engineering (DHSE). This achievement was not just a personal triumph but a contribution to the healthcare system, where technology and health care intersect to improve lives.

My story is a tapestry of struggle, adaptation, and triumph. It's a journey of a young Eritrean who dared to dream, traversed continents, bridged cultures, and found his purpose in the fusion of technology and healthcare. It's a narrative of breaking barriers, embracing new beginnings, and tirelessly working towards a future where technology enhances health and well-being.

CONTENTS

Introduction

Welcome to the intriguing world of Wealth Psychology! In this chapter, we embark on a journey that explores the profound connection between our minds and our financial well-being. As you delve into the pages of this book, you'll discover the fascinating interplay of thoughts, emotions, beliefs, and behaviors that shape our relationship with wealth and money.

Money is more than just currency; it's a powerful force that influences every aspect of our lives. It can open doors to opportunities, provide security and comfort, and enable us to pursue our dreams. But it can also be a source of stress, anxiety, and conflict. Our attitudes and behaviors towards money are deeply rooted in our psychology, often shaped by our upbringing, experiences, and the values we hold dear.

Wealth Psychology is about understanding this intricate dance between our inner world and the external world of finance. It's about recognizing the subconscious beliefs that drive our financial decisions, both big and small. It's about uncovering the emotional triggers that lead to impulsive spending or hesitancy in investing. It's about embracing the mindset and behaviors that can help you build and manage wealth in a way that aligns with your values and aspirations.

Throughout this book, we will explore a wide range of topics, from the impact of childhood experiences on our money mindset to the psychology of investments, from the role of gratitude in wealth to strategies for overcoming financial stress. We'll discuss how our relationship with money affects our relationships with others, including our partners and family members. We'll also delve into the emotional aspects of financial decision-making, such as regret, fear, and the joy of financial independence.

Wealth Psychology is not just about accumulating wealth for its own sake. It's about achieving a harmonious and fulfilling relationship with money that empowers you to live the life you desire. It's about recognizing that wealth is not solely defined by numbers in a bank account but by the sense of security, happiness, and purpose it brings.

Throughout this journey, you'll find practical insights, exercises, and Real-life stories that illustrate the principles of Wealth Psychology. By the End of this book, you'll have a deeper understanding of your own financial mindset and the tools to make more informed, intentional, and empowering financial choices.

So, let's embark on this exploration of Wealth Psychology together. Whether you're seeking to build wealth, overcome financial challenges, or simply gain a deeper understanding of your financial behaviors, you'll find valuable insights and guidance within these pages. Prepare to unlock the hidden potential within your relationship with money and embark on a path towards a more prosperous and fulfilling life.

Chapter 1

The Mindset of Wealth

Welcome to the fascinating journey of exploring the Mindset of Wealth. In this chapter, we'll delve into the foundational aspects of our thinking and beliefs surrounding wealth and money. You'll discover that building wealth isn't just about earning a high income; it begins with cultivating the right mindset and understanding the psychological factors that influence our financial decisions.

The Power of Mindset

Your mindset is like the compass that guides your financial journey. It shapes your attitudes and behaviors toward money and ultimately determines your financial success or challenges. Developing a wealth mindset is the first step toward achieving financial abundance.

Abundance vs. Scarcity Mindset

One of the fundamental concepts in wealth psychology is the distinction between an abundance mindset and a scarcity mindset. Those with an abundance mindset believe that opportunities are limitless, and there's enough wealth to go around for everyone. On the other hand, individuals with a scarcity mindset tend to believe that resources are scarce, and they constantly fear running out of money.

Cultivating an abundance mindset involves shifting your focus from what you lack to what you have and what you can create. It's about seeing opportunities rather than obstacles and believing in your ability to generate wealth.

The Influence of beliefs

Our beliefs about money are often deeply ingrained from childhood and can have a profound impact on our financial decisions. For example, if you grew up hearing phrases like "money is the root of all evil" or "rich people are greedy," these beliefs can create internal conflicts and hinder your financial growth.

Take some time to reflect on your own money beliefs. Are they empowering or limiting? Recognizing and challenging limiting beliefs is a crucial step in developing a wealth mindset.

Financial Self-Efficacy

Another essential aspect of the mindset of wealth is financial self-efficacy, which is your belief in your ability to manage money effectively and achieve financial goals. People with high financial self-efficacy are more likely to take initiative in their financial lives and persevere through challenges.

Building Financial Confidence

Building financial self-efficacy starts with gaining knowledge and skills in money management. Educate yourself about budgeting, investing, and financial planning. Seek out resources, courses, or advisors who can help you develop financial competence.

Setting and Achieving Financial Goals

Goal setting is a powerful tool for cultivating a wealth mindset. When you set clear and achievable financial goals, you create a sense of purpose and direction in your financial life. Start by defining your short-term and long-term financial objectives and break them down into actionable steps.

The Role of Gratitude

Gratitude is a cornerstone of the wealth mindset. It's about appreciating what you have and acknowledging your financial progress. Cultivating gratitude can shift your focus away from what you lack and toward the abundance already present in your life.

Gratitude Practices

Consider incorporating gratitude practices into your daily life. Keep a gratitude journal, where you write down three things you're grateful for each day. This simple habit can help rewire your brain to focus on abundance.

Conclusion

In this chapter, we've explored the fundamental aspects of the mindset of wealth. It's not just about accumulating wealth for its own sake; it's about developing the right attitudes, beliefs, and confidence to navigate your financial journey successfully. As you continue your exploration of Wealth Psychology, remember that your mindset is the compass that will guide you toward a more prosperous and fulfilling financial future. In the chapters ahead, we'll delve deeper into the psychology of money and provide practical strategies for building and managing wealth while nurturing a positive and empowering mindset.

Chapter 2

Understanding Your Money beliefs

We'll explore the intricate web of money beliefs that have been shaping your financial decisions for years, if not decades. Understanding these beliefs is a crucial step in transforming your relationship with money and building lasting wealth.

The Foundation of Money beliefs

Our beliefs about money are like the invisible scaffolding that supports our financial decisions. These beliefs often form during childhood and are influenced by our family, culture, and personal experiences. They can be both empowering and limiting, and recognizing their influence is the first step toward change.

Exploring Your Money History

To understand your money beliefs, it's essential to take a journey into your personal money history. Reflect on the following questions:

- What were the money conversations like in your family when you were growing up?

- Were you taught that money is a source of security or stress?

- Did you witness any significant financial events that left a lasting impression?

- How did your caregivers approach saving, spending, and investing?

These reflections can reveal the roots of your current money beliefs and offer insights into why you make certain financial choices today.

Common Money Belief Systems

Money beliefs come in various forms, and they can profoundly influence your financial behavior. Let's explore some common money belief systems:

Scarcity vs. Abundance Beliefs

As mentioned in the previous chapter, individuals with scarcity beliefs often worry about running out of money, leading to frugality or a fear of taking financial risks. Those with abundance beliefs, on the other hand, tend to believe in the limitless potential for wealth.

Money as a Measure of Self-Worth

Many people tie their self-worth to their financial success. If you believe that your value as a person is determined by your income or assets, it can lead to feelings of inadequacy and anxiety.

Fear of Money

Some individuals have a deep-seated fear of money, often stemming from negative experiences or beliefs that wealth leads to negative consequences. This fear can manifest as self-sabotage in financial matters.

Money as Freedom

On the positive side, some people see money as a tool for achieving freedom and fulfilling their dreams. They believe that financial success can lead to a life of choice and opportunity.

Identifying Your Money beliefs

Now that you have a sense of the various money belief systems, it's time to identify your own beliefs. Engage in self-reflection and journaling to uncover your money beliefs. Pay attention to your emotional reactions when you think about money and consider consulting with a therapist or financial coach if you find it challenging to explore these beliefs on your own.

Challenging and Changing Your Money beliefs

Once you've identified your money beliefs, it's important to evaluate whether they serve you well or hold you back. Remember that beliefs are not set in stone; they can be challenged and changed over time.

Questioning Limiting beliefs

Ask yourself whether your money beliefs are based on facts or assumptions. Challenge beliefs that limit your financial growth by seeking evidence to the contrary. Surround yourself with positive and supportive influences that reinforce healthier beliefs.

Positive Affirmations

Positive affirmations can be a powerful tool for shifting your money mindset. Create affirmations that counteract negative beliefs and repeat them daily to reinforce positive thinking.

Seeking Professional Help

If you find it challenging to overcome deeply ingrained money beliefs, consider working with a therapist or financial coach who specializes in money psychology. They can provide guidance and strategies for transformation.

Conclusion

Understanding your money beliefs is a significant step in your journey toward financial empowerment. By recognizing the influence of these beliefs and actively working to reshape them, you can lay the foundation for a healthier and more abundant relationship with money. In the chapters ahead, we'll continue to explore the psychology of wealth and provide practical strategies for harnessing the power of your money beliefs to achieve your financial goals and aspirations.

Chapter 3

Overcoming Financial Limitations

We'll delve into the practical steps and strategies for overcoming the financial limitations that may be holding you back from achieving your wealth and financial goals. By addressing these limitations head-on, you'll pave the way for a more prosperous future.

Identifying Your Financial Limitations

Financial limitations can take various forms, and they often lurk beneath the surface, affecting your decisions without you even realizing it. It's crucial to identify these limitations before you can effectively overcome them.

Common Financial Limitations

1. Self-Doubt: Feeling uncertain or lacking confidence in your ability to manage money or make sound financial decisions.

2. Procrastination: Putting off important financial tasks or decisions, which can lead to missed opportunities or financial stress.

3. Impulse Control: Struggling with impulse spending, often driven by emotional triggers rather than rational decision-making.

4. Financial Ignorance: Lacking knowledge about basic financial concepts, leading to poor money management choices.

5. Fear of Risk: Avoiding investments or financial opportunities due to a fear of losing money, even if they have the potential for significant returns.

6. Debt Overwhelm: Feeling trapped by debt and unable to make progress towards paying it off.

7. Comparison Trap: Constantly comparing your financial situation to others, leading to feelings of inadequacy or unworthiness.

8. Lack of Financial Goals: Not having clear financial objectives, which can result in drifting aimlessly in your financial life.

Strategies for Overcoming Financial Limitations

Now that you have a better understanding of the potential limitations you may be facing, let's explore some practical strategies for overcoming them.

1. Self-Awareness and Mindfulness

Start by becoming more aware of your financial thoughts and behaviors. Mindfulness techniques can help you recognize your impulses and emotional triggers when it comes to money. By being present in the moment, you can make more deliberate and conscious financial decisions.

2. Financial Education

Address financial ignorance by investing in your financial education. There are numerous resources available, from books and online courses to workshops and financial advisors. Take the initiative to learn about budgeting, investing, and other essential financial topics.

3. Setting Clear Financial Goals

Having specific, measurable, and achievable financial goals can provide a sense of purpose and direction. Whether it's paying off debt, saving for retirement, or starting a business, setting goals helps you stay motivated and focused.

4. Budgeting and Financial Planning

Creating a budget and financial plan can help you take control of your finances. Track your income and expenses, identify areas for saving, and allocate funds towards your financial goals. Consistent budgeting can alleviate financial stress.

5. Seek Professional Guidance

If you're overwhelmed by debt or feel uncertain about financial decisions, consider seeking the help of a financial advisor or counselor.

They can provide personalized guidance and strategies tailored to your situation.

6. Embrace Risk in a Controlled Manner

Don't let fear of financial risk paralyze you. While it's essential to make informed decisions, some level of risk is often necessary for financial growth. Diversifying your investments and seeking professional advice can help you manage risk effectively.

7. Practice Delayed Gratification

Overcoming impulse control issues can be challenging but rewarding. Practice delaying gratification by setting a waiting period before making significant purchases. This gives you time to consider whether the purchase aligns with your financial goals.

Conclusion

Financial limitations are not insurmountable obstacles; they are challenges that can be overcome with patience, awareness, and action. By identifying and addressing these limitations, you can take control of your financial future and work towards building the wealth and financial security you desire. In the chapters ahead, we will continue to explore the psychology of money and provide further guidance on achieving your financial aspirations while nurturing a positive and empowering mindset.

Chapter 4

The Psychology of Money Goals

Where we delve into the fascinating world of setting and achieving money goals. Money goals are not just about accumulating wealth; they are a powerful tool for shaping your financial future and bringing your dreams to life. In this chapter, we will explore the psychology behind money goals and provide you with practical strategies to set and accomplish them effectively.

The Significance of Money Goals

Money goals serve as the North Star of your financial journey. They provide direction, motivation, and a sense of purpose in your financial decisions. Understanding why you want to achieve these goals is just as important as the goals themselves.

Financial Dreams and Aspirations

Start by envisioning your financial dreams and aspirations. What does financial success mean to you? It could be buying a home, traveling the world, starting a business, or ensuring a comfortable retirement. These dreams form the basis of your money goals.

Motivation and Purpose

Having a clear sense of purpose behind your money goals can be a powerful motivator. Knowing that your goals will enable you to provide for your family, support a cause you care about, or achieve personal fulfillment can drive you to take consistent action.

SMART Money Goals

Effective money goals are SMART: Specific, Measurable, Achievable, Relevant, and Time-bound. Let's break down these components:

Specific

Your goals should be well-defined and clear. Instead of saying, "I want to save money," specify the exact amount and purpose, such as "I want to save $10,000 for a down payment on a house in two years."

Measurable

Include a way to measure your progress. This helps you track how close you are to achieving your goal and stay motivated. For example, "I will save $500 per month."

Achievable

Your goals should be realistic and attainable within your current financial situation. Set yourself up for success by ensuring your goals are within reach.

Relevant

Align your goals with your values and long-term objectives. Ensure that achieving these goals will have a meaningful impact on your life.

Time-bound

Set a deadline for achieving your goals. A timeline creates a sense of urgency and helps you stay on track. For instance, "I will save $10,000 for a down payment on a house in two years."

The Psychology of Goal Setting

Understanding the psychology behind goal setting can help you overcome common challenges and stay committed to your objectives.

Visualize Your Success

Use visualization techniques to picture yourself achieving your goals. Imagine the emotions, experiences, and rewards associated with success. This can reinforce your commitment to your goals.

Break Down Your Goals

Large goals can be intimidating, so break them into smaller, manageable steps. Each step you complete brings you closer to your ultimate goal, creating a sense of accomplishment along the way.

Accountability and Support

Share your goals with a trusted friend or family member who can provide encouragement and hold you accountable. Accountability can be a powerful motivator.

Stay Flexible

Life is unpredictable, and circumstances can change. Be open to adjusting your goals as needed. Adaptability is a key trait of successful goal achievers.

Celebrate Your Achievements

Finally, remember to celebrate your achievements along the way. Recognize and reward yourself for reaching milestones. Celebrating your progress reinforces the positive feelings associated with goal accomplishment.

Conclusion

Setting and achieving money goals is a journey of self-discovery and empowerment. By understanding the psychology behind goal setting and applying the principles of SMART goals, you can create a roadmap to financial success that aligns with your dreams and aspirations. In the chapters ahead, we'll continue to explore the psychology of wealth and provide further guidance on managing your finances while nurturing a positive and empowering mindset.

Chapter 5

Wealth and Happiness

We will explore the intricate relationship between wealth and happiness, a topic that has fascinated humanity for centuries. While wealth alone may not guarantee happiness, understanding the connection between the two can help you make informed decisions about your financial well-being and overall life satisfaction.

The Pursuit of Happiness

As individuals, we all seek happiness and contentment in our lives. The pursuit of happiness is a universal goal that transcends cultural and socioeconomic boundaries. However, it's essential to recognize that happiness is a complex and multifaceted concept, and its relationship with wealth is not always straightforward.

The Role of Wealth in Life Satisfaction

Numerous studies have explored the correlation between wealth and life satisfaction. While wealth can contribute to happiness to some extent, its impact varies among individuals and depends on various factors.

Basic Needs and Financial Security

Wealth plays a significant role in meeting basic needs and providing financial security. Having access to necessities such as food, shelter, healthcare, and education can lead to a higher quality of life and, consequently, increased happiness.

Beyond the Basics

However, beyond a certain point where basic needs are met, the relationship between wealth and happiness becomes more complex. Research suggests that the pursuit of material wealth alone may not lead to sustained happiness.

The Hedonic Treadmill

One psychological phenomenon that explains the complexities of wealth and happiness is the hedonic treadmill. This theory suggests that people tend to adapt to changes in their circumstances, including increases in income and wealth. As a result, the initial boost in happiness from acquiring more wealth tends to be temporary, and individuals often revert to their baseline level of happiness.

The Impact of Lifestyle Inflation

Lifestyle inflation occurs when people increase their spending as their income rises. While this can lead to temporary pleasures and comforts, it may not necessarily result in lasting happiness. Recognizing and managing lifestyle inflation is crucial for maintaining a healthy relationship between wealth and happiness.

Beyond Material Wealth

To find enduring happiness, it's essential to look beyond material wealth and consider other factors that contribute to well-being.

Positive Psychology

Positive psychology emphasizes the importance of factors such as gratitude, optimism, meaningful relationships, and personal growth in fostering happiness. These elements of well-being are not solely dependent on financial wealth but can be nurtured and cultivated regardless of your financial situation.

Purpose and Meaning

Finding purpose and meaning in life can have a profound impact on happiness. Engaging in activities that align with your values and contribute to a greater good can lead to a sense of fulfillment that transcends material wealth.

Social Connections

Strong social connections and a supportive network of friends and family are consistently linked to higher levels of happiness.

Investing time and effort in nurturing these relationships can significantly enhance your overall well-being.

Financial Goals and Happiness

The key to integrating wealth and happiness lies in setting meaningful financial goals that align with your values and contribute to your overall life satisfaction. Rather than pursuing wealth for its own sake, consider how it can enable you to live a life that brings you joy and fulfillment.

Conclusion

Wealth and happiness are intertwined but not synonymous. While wealth can enhance certain aspects of life satisfaction, it is only one piece of the happiness puzzle. Understanding the complexities of this relationship empowers you to make informed financial decisions that prioritize your well-being and align with your values and goals.

In the chapters ahead, we'll continue to explore the psychology of wealth and provide guidance on achieving financial success while nurturing a positive and fulfilling life.

Chapter 6

The Role of Self-Esteem in Wealth

We delve into the profound connection between self-esteem and wealth. Your self-esteem, the way you perceive and value yourself, plays a pivotal role in shaping your financial choices and overall financial well-being. In this chapter, we will explore how self-esteem influences your relationship with money and provides insights on how to nurture a healthy sense of self-worth for financial success.

Understanding Self-Esteem

Self-esteem is the foundation of your self-concept. It reflects your beliefs about your worthiness, capabilities, and deservingness of success and happiness. Healthy self-esteem is characterized by a positive self-image and a sense of self-worth that is not dependent on external validation.

The Impact of Self-Esteem on Financial Decisions

Self-esteem profoundly influences your financial choices, as it shapes your beliefs and behaviors surrounding money. Here's how self-esteem can affect your financial life:

1. Self-Worth and Money

People with healthy self-esteem tend to believe they deserve financial success and are more likely to make decisions that lead to wealth accumulation. In contrast, low self-esteem can manifest as self-sabotage or reluctance to pursue financial opportunities.

2. Risk Tolerance

Self-esteem influences your willingness to take financial risks. Individuals with high self-esteem are more likely to embrace calculated risks and investment opportunities, while those with low self-esteem may fear failure and avoid such opportunities.

3. Financial Self-Care

Caring for your financial well-being is an act of self-respect. People with high self-esteem are more likely to engage in financial self-care practices, such as budgeting, saving, and investing, as they value themselves and their future.

4. Relationships and Money

Self-esteem also affects how you handle financial aspects of your relationships. People with healthy self-esteem are better equipped to set boundaries, communicate openly about money, and make financial decisions that benefit both themselves and their partners.

Nurturing Healthy Self-Esteem for Financial Success

Building and maintaining healthy self-esteem is an ongoing process that can positively impact your financial life. Here are some strategies to nurture your self-esteem:

1. Self-Reflection

Take time to reflect on your beliefs and thoughts about money. Identify any negative beliefs or self-criticisms related to your financial situation, and work on reframing them into more positive and empowering statements.

2. Self-Care

Prioritize self-care to boost your self-esteem. Engage in activities that make you feel good about yourself, both physically and mentally. Exercise, meditation, and self-compassion practices can help.

3. Seek Support

Consider seeking support from a therapist or counselor if you have deep-seated self-esteem issues that are negatively impacting your financial decisions. Professional guidance can be transformative.

4. Set Achievable Financial Goals

Setting and achieving financial goals can boost your self-esteem. Each success reinforces your sense of capability and self-worth. Start with small, achievable goals and gradually work your way up.

5. Surround Yourself with Positivity

Surround yourself with people who uplift and support you. Limit exposure to negative influences that can erode your self-esteem, whether they be people, media, or social networks.

Conclusion

Your self-esteem is a crucial factor in your financial well-being and overall quality of life. Recognizing its influence on your relationship with money and taking proactive steps to nurture healthy self-esteem can empower you to make more informed and positive financial decisions.

In the chapters ahead, we will continue to explore the psychology of wealth and provide guidance on achieving financial success while fostering a strong sense of self-worth and fulfillment.

Chapter 7

Money and Personal Values

Your values serve as the compass that guides your financial decisions and shapes your overall life satisfaction. In this chapter, we will delve into the influence of personal values on your financial choices and provide insights on aligning your money decisions with what truly matters to you.

Understanding Personal Values

Personal values are the principles, beliefs, and ideals that define what is important and meaningful to you. They reflect your priorities and guide your choices in various aspects of life, including your financial decisions.

The Impact of Personal Values on Money Choices

Your personal values have a significant influence on how you earn, spend, save, and invest your money. Here's how they shape your financial life:

1. Spending and Lifestyle Choices

Your values determine where you allocate your resources. For example, if family is a core value, you may prioritize spending on family vacations or educational opportunities for your children. If environmental sustainability is important to you, you may choose eco-friendly products and support companies with sustainable practices.

2. Career and Income

Your values can influence your career choices and income goals. If personal growth and creativity are fundamental values, you may seek out a career that allows for self-expression and continuous learning. Alternatively, if financial security is a top value, you might prioritize job stability and a steady income.

3. Saving and Investing

Your values also play a role in your saving and investing strategies. If your long-term goal is to support charitable causes, you may set aside a portion of your income for philanthropic endeavors. Alternatively, if financial independence is a core value, you might prioritize investments that yield long-term financial growth.

Aligning Money with Values

Achieving financial well-being involves aligning your financial decisions with your personal values. Here are steps to help you bring your money and values into harmony:

1. Identify Your Core Values

Take time to reflect on your values. What truly matters to you? Create a list of your core values, whether they involve family, personal growth, environmental responsibility, or other principles that resonate with you.

2. Prioritize Your Values

Once you've identified your values, prioritize them based on their significance in your life. Clarify which values are most essential to you and which may be secondary.

3. Set Financial Goals

Align your financial goals with your core values. For each value, consider specific financial objectives that reflect its importance. For example, if health is a core value, set goals related to fitness, nutrition, and healthcare spending.

4. Review and Adjust Your Financial Choices

Regularly review your financial decisions to ensure they align with your values and goals. If you find that your spending or investment choices are incongruent with your values, consider adjustments that bring them into harmony.

5. Seek Professional Guidance

A financial advisor or planner can help you develop a financial plan that aligns with your values and long-term objectives. They can provide guidance on investment strategies, budgeting, and achieving your financial goals while staying true to your values.

Conclusion

Understanding the relationship between money and personal values is a vital aspect of achieving financial fulfillment and overall life satisfaction. When your financial decisions align with what truly matters to you, you create a sense of purpose and authenticity in your financial life.

In the chapters ahead, we will continue to explore the psychology of wealth and provide guidance on achieving financial success while nurturing a deep connection with your values and aspirations.

Chapter 8

Financial Planning

And

Psychological Well-being

The transformative relationship between financial planning and psychological well-being. The way you manage your finances can profoundly impact your mental and emotional health, and this chapter explores how thoughtful financial planning can enhance your overall sense of well-being.

The Intersection of Finances and Mental Health

Financial planning is not just about managing numbers; it's about nurturing your psychological well-being. Your financial situation can significantly influence your mental and emotional health. Let's explore how these aspects are intertwined:

1. Financial Stress and Mental Health

Financial stress is a common source of anxiety and depression. The burden of debt, job insecurity, or insufficient savings can take a toll on your mental well-being. Developing a sound financial plan can help alleviate this stress and create a sense of control over your financial future.

2. Goal Achievement and Self-Esteem

Setting and achieving financial goals can boost your self-esteem and overall life satisfaction. Each milestone you reach reinforces your sense of accomplishment and contributes to your psychological well-being.

3. Financial Security and Peace of Mind

Having a financial safety net, such as an emergency fund and insurance, provides peace of mind in times of uncertainty. Knowing you have a plan in place for unexpected expenses or life changes can reduce anxiety and improve your mental well-being.

4. Financial Harmony in Relationships

Money issues are a common source of conflict in relationships. Effective financial planning can foster open communication, trust, and alignment with your partner, contributing to healthier and more satisfying relationships.

The Benefits of Financial Planning for Psychological Well-being

1. Reduced Anxiety

A well-thought-out financial plan provides clarity and structure, reducing financial uncertainty and anxiety. Knowing you have a roadmap to achieve your financial goals can ease worries about the future.

2. Increased Confidence

Financial planning instills confidence in your ability to manage your money effectively. As you make informed decisions and see progress toward your goals, your self-assurance grows.

3. Enhanced Decision-Making

A financial plan guides your decision-making, helping you prioritize your financial goals and allocate resources wisely. This sense of purpose can improve your overall decision-making abilities.

4. Greater Resilience

Having a financial plan in place can enhance your resilience in the face of financial setbacks. It provides a framework for navigating challenges and bouncing back from adversity.

5. Improved Relationships

Effective financial planning fosters open communication and trust in relationships. It allows you to collaborate with your partner or family members on financial goals, leading to more harmonious interactions.

Developing a Personal Financial Plan

To leverage the benefits of financial planning for your psychological well-being, consider these steps:

1. Set Clear Financial Goals

Define your financial goals and objectives, whether they involve saving for retirement, paying off debt, or funding a dream vacation. Be specific, measurable, and time bound.

2. Create a Budget

Develop a budget that outlines your income and expenses. This will help you understand your financial inflows and outflows, identify areas for savings, and stay on track with your goals.

3. Build an Emergency Fund

Prioritize the creation of an emergency fund to provide financial security during unexpected events. Having a safety net can significantly reduce anxiety and stress.

4. Invest Wisely

Explore investment options that align with your financial goals and risk tolerance. Diversifying your investments can help you achieve long-term financial growth and peace of mind.

5. Seek Professional Guidance

Consider working with a financial advisor or planner who can provide expert guidance and tailor a financial plan to your unique circumstances and aspirations.

Conclusion

Financial planning is not just about managing money; it's about enhancing your psychological well-being. By developing a sound financial plan and aligning your financial decisions with your goals and values, you can reduce financial stress, boost your confidence, and foster greater peace of mind.

In the chapters ahead, we will continue to explore the psychology of wealth and provide guidance on achieving financial success while nurturing your mental and emotional health.

Chapter 9

Wealth and Emotional Intelligence

The fascinating connection between wealth and emotional intelligence. Emotional intelligence, often abbreviated as EQ, is a critical factor in achieving financial success and maintaining a balanced and fulfilling life. In this chapter, we'll delve into how emotional intelligence influences your financial decisions and overall well-being.

The Role of Emotional Intelligence

Emotional intelligence encompasses the ability to recognize, understand, manage, and effectively use emotions in various aspects of life. It involves both self-awareness and the capacity to navigate social interactions skillfully.

Emotional Intelligence and Wealth

Emotional intelligence has a profound impact on your financial choices and outcomes. Here's how EQ influences your relationship with wealth:

1. Self-Regulation

Individuals with high emotional intelligence can manage their impulses, especially when it comes to financial decisions. They are less likely to make impulsive or emotionally driven financial choices that can lead to debt or financial stress.

2. Decision-Making

Emotional intelligence enhances your ability to make informed and rational financial decisions. It allows you to assess risks, consider long-term consequences, and resist the temptation of quick fixes or get-rich-quick schemes.

3. Communication and Negotiation

Effective communication is crucial in financial matters, whether in negotiations, investments, or discussions with financial advisors. High EQ individuals excel in conveying their needs, understanding others' perspectives, and reaching mutually beneficial financial agreements.

4. Resilience

Emotional intelligence enhances resilience in the face of financial setbacks. It helps individuals bounce back from financial challenges, learn from their experiences, and adapt to changing circumstances.

Developing Emotional Intelligence for Wealth

To harness the benefits of emotional intelligence in your financial life, consider these strategies:

1. Self-Awareness

Begin by developing self-awareness. Reflect on your emotional reactions to financial situations. Are you prone to anxiety, impulsivity, or fear when dealing with money? Identifying these patterns is the first step toward improving your EQ.

2. Self-Regulation

Practice self-regulation by learning to manage your emotions in financial decisions. Take a pause when facing a major financial choice to ensure it's not driven by fear or greed. Engage in relaxation techniques, such as deep breathing or mindfulness, to stay calm and focused.

3. Empathy

Cultivate empathy, which is the ability to understand and share the feelings of others. This skill can enhance your relationships with financial advisors, partners, and colleagues, leading to more collaborative and successful financial outcomes.

4. Effective Communication

Enhance your communication skills by actively listening and expressing your thoughts and feelings clearly. Effective communication is essential when discussing financial goals, strategies, or challenges.

5. Conflict Resolution

Learn conflict resolution techniques to navigate financial disagreements constructively. These skills can prevent financial conflicts from escalating and jeopardizing your financial well-being.

6. Adaptability

Develop adaptability to navigate the ever-changing financial landscape. Being open to new information, strategies, and financial opportunities can lead to better financial outcomes.

Conclusion

Emotional intelligence is a valuable asset in your journey toward financial success and personal well-being. By enhancing your EQ, you can make more informed and rational financial decisions, build stronger relationships, and navigate financial challenges with resilience.

In the chapters ahead, we will continue to explore the psychology of wealth and provide guidance on achieving financial success while nurturing your emotional intelligence for a more fulfilling life.

Chapter 10

The Influence of Childhood on Wealth Psychology

The profound impact of childhood experiences on your wealth psychology. Your early experiences and upbringing play a significant role in shaping your beliefs, attitudes, and behaviors related to money and wealth. In this chapter, we'll delve into the intricate ways in which childhood influences your financial mindset and provide insights on understanding and transforming these influences.

The Foundation of Money beliefs

1. Family Dynamics

Your family is often the primary source of your early money beliefs. Observe how your parents or caregivers managed money, their attitudes toward wealth, and the financial lessons they imparted. These observations can shape your own financial values and habits.

2. Money Messages

Reflect on the explicit and implicit messages you received about money during your upbringing. Did your family emphasize the importance of saving, investing, and financial security? Or were there negative beliefs about money, such as it being a source of conflict or stress?

3. Early Financial Experiences

Consider your early financial experiences, such as receiving an allowance, opening your first bank account, or making your first purchase. These experiences can influence your attitudes and emotions related to money.

The Impact of Childhood Experiences on Wealth Psychology

1. Money Mindset

Your early experiences contribute to your money mindset, which includes your beliefs about wealth, abundance, scarcity, and your own worthiness to achieve financial success. For example, growing up in an environment of financial security can lead to a more positive money mindset, while childhood experiences of financial instability may result in a scarcity mindset.

2. Financial Habits

Your childhood experiences also shape your financial habits and behaviors. If you witnessed responsible money management at home, you are more likely to adopt similar habits. Conversely, if you grew up in an environment of financial chaos, you may struggle with financial discipline as an adult.

3. Emotional Associations

Childhood experiences can create emotional associations with money. Positive experiences related to money may lead to feelings of security and confidence, while negative experiences can trigger emotions like fear, guilt, or shame.

Understanding and Transforming Childhood Influences

1. Self-Reflection

Engage in self-reflection to gain insight into the influence of childhood experiences on your current financial mindset and behaviors. Consider keeping a journal to explore your beliefs, emotions, and habits related to money.

2. Seek Professional Guidance

If childhood experiences have left deep-seated emotional wounds or negative beliefs about money, consider seeking the help of a therapist or counselor who specializes in money psychology. They can provide support and strategies for healing and transformation.

3. Reevaluate and Relearn

Challenge and reevaluate any limiting beliefs or unhelpful financial habits that may have originated from childhood experiences. Replace them with empowering beliefs and constructive financial behaviors.

4. Create New Financial Narratives

Develop new narratives about money that align with your current values and financial goals. These narratives can serve as the foundation for a healthier and more empowered relationship with money.

Conclusion

Childhood experiences hold a powerful influence on your wealth psychology, but they do not determine your financial future. By understanding and transforming the impact of these early experiences, you can take control of your financial mindset and behaviors, shaping a more positive and fulfilling relationship with money.

In the chapters ahead, we will continue to explore the psychology of wealth and provide guidance on achieving financial success while nurturing a mindset that empowers your financial well-being.

Chapter 11

Your Relationship with Money

Where we'll embark on a journey to explore your personal relationship with money. Your connection with money is complex and deeply rooted in your beliefs, experiences, and emotions. In this chapter, we'll dive into the intricacies of this relationship, helping you gain insight and foster a healthier, more empowering connection with your finances.

The Multifaceted Nature of Your Relationship with Money

1. Beliefs and Attitudes

Your beliefs and attitudes about money serve as the foundation of your relationship with it. These beliefs can encompass notions of abundance, scarcity, deservingness, and the role of money in your life.

2. Emotional Associations

Money often triggers strong emotions. It can evoke feelings of security, anxiety, guilt, pleasure, or even shame. Exploring your emotional responses to money is a crucial step in understanding your relationship with it.

3. Past Experiences

Past financial experiences, both positive and negative, shape your relationship with money. Reflect on how these experiences have influenced your current financial decisions and behaviors.

The Impact of Your Relationship with Money

1. Financial Habits

Your relationship with money plays a pivotal role in determining your financial habits and behaviors. It influences how you save, spend, invest, and manage your finances on a daily basis.

2. Financial Goals

Your beliefs and emotions regarding money can either propel you toward your financial goals or hinder your progress. Understanding your relationship with money is essential for setting and achieving these goals effectively.

3. Decision-Making

Financial decisions, whether minor or major, are deeply influenced by your relationship with money. It affects your choices in areas like career, investments, lifestyle, and philanthropy.

Reflecting on Your Relationship with Money

To gain a deeper understanding of your relationship with money, consider the following exercises:

1. Money Journaling

Keep a money journal to record your thoughts, beliefs, and emotions related to money. Document your financial decisions and their underlying motivations.

2. Self-Assessment

Reflect on your financial habits and behaviors. Are you a spender or a saver? Do you approach investments cautiously or take calculated risks? Analyze how your relationship with money influences these tendencies.

3. Childhood Reflection

Examine the role of childhood experiences in shaping your current relationship with money. Consider the financial messages you received from your family and the emotions associated with money during your upbringing.

Nurturing a Healthier Relationship with Money

1. Self-Compassion

Practice self-compassion when exploring your relationship with money. Recognize that everyone has a unique financial journey with both strengths and challenges.

2. Challenge Limiting beliefs

Identify any limiting beliefs or negative associations with money that may be holding you back. Challenge these beliefs and replace them with more empowering ones.

3. Embrace Financial Education

Invest in financial education to expand your knowledge and confidence in managing money. The more you understand the financial world, the more empowered you become in your decisions.

4. Seek Professional Guidance

Consider consulting a financial advisor or therapist specializing in money psychology if you're facing deep-seated financial issues or emotional challenges related to money. They can provide tailored guidance and support.

Conclusion

Your relationship with money is a dynamic and evolving aspect of your life. By exploring and nurturing this relationship, you can transform it into a source of empowerment, helping you make sound financial decisions and achieve your financial goals. In the chapters ahead, we will continue to explore the psychology of wealth and provide guidance on achieving financial success while nurturing a healthy and positive connection with money.

Chapter 12

Cognitive Biases in Wealth Decisions

We'll unravel the intriguing world of cognitive biases and their profound impact on your wealth decisions. Cognitive biases are the quirks in human thinking that can lead to irrational judgments and choices, including those related to money and wealth. In this chapter, we'll delve into these biases, helping you recognize and navigate them more effectively to make wiser financial decisions.

Understanding Cognitive Biases

1. Anchoring Bias

The anchoring bias occurs when individuals rely too heavily on the first piece of information encountered (the "anchor") when making decisions. In wealth decisions, this bias can lead to overvaluing initial offers or prices, which may not be in your best financial interest.

2. Confirmation Bias

Confirmation bias involves seeking, interpreting, and remembering information that confirms your existing beliefs or decisions. In financial matters, it can lead to overlooking crucial information that challenges your financial choices.

3. Loss Aversion

Loss aversion refers to the tendency to strongly prefer avoiding losses over acquiring equivalent gains. This bias can lead to overly conservative financial decisions, causing you to miss out on potentially beneficial opportunities.

4. Overconfidence Bias

Overconfidence bias results in individuals overestimating their own abilities and knowledge. When it comes to wealth decisions, this bias can lead to excessive risk-taking or unwarranted certainty about investment outcomes.

5. Sunk Cost Fallacy

The sunk cost fallacy occurs when individuals continue investing in a decision or project based on the resources (time, money, effort) already invested, even when it's no longer a rational choice. In wealth management, this can lead to holding onto underperforming investments or assets.

6. Herd Mentality

Herd mentality involves following the crowd or conforming to the behavior of others without critical evaluation. In the financial world, this bias can lead to speculative bubbles and market crashes.

Recognizing and Navigating Cognitive Biases

1. Self-Awareness

The first step in overcoming cognitive biases is self-awareness. Recognize that everyone is susceptible to biases, and being aware of their existence is essential for making more rational decisions.

2. Slow Down and Reflect

Take your time when making important wealth decisions. Slow down the decision-making process to carefully consider all available information and potential biases that may be affecting your judgment.

3. Seek Diverse Perspectives

Encourage diverse viewpoints when making financial choices. Consulting with financial advisors or seeking input from trusted individuals with different perspectives can help counteract biases.

4. Embrace Evidence-Based Decision-Making

Prioritize evidence-based decision-making over intuition or gut feelings. Seek empirical data and research to inform your financial choices.

5. Set Clear Decision-Making Criteria

Establish clear decision-making criteria in advance. Define your financial goals and criteria for success, which can help mitigate the influence of biases.

6. Monitor and Reflect

Regularly review your financial decisions and outcomes. Assess whether any biases may have influenced your choices and adjust your decision-making process accordingly.

Conclusion

Cognitive biases are an inherent part of human thinking, but they need not dictate your financial decisions. By recognizing these biases and implementing strategies to counteract them, you can make more rational, informed, and ultimately, more successful wealth decisions.

In the chapters ahead, we will continue to explore the psychology of wealth and provide guidance on achieving financial success while navigating the intricacies of the human mind.

Chapter 13

The Fear of Wealth

Where we'll delve into a fascinating and often overlooked aspect of wealth psychology—the fear of wealth. While many people aspire to accumulate wealth, there are those who harbor deep-seated fears and anxieties associated with financial success. In this chapter, we'll explore the roots of this fear, its consequences, and strategies for addressing and overcoming it.

Understanding the Fear of Wealth

1. Fear of Responsibility

Some individuals fear the responsibilities that come with wealth, such as managing investments, making financial decisions, and dealing with increased tax complexities. This fear can stem from a lack of financial literacy or confidence in handling wealth-related matters.

2. Fear of Change

Wealth often entails significant life changes, including shifts in social circles, lifestyle adjustments, and new financial considerations. The fear of change can be a barrier to pursuing wealth, as individuals may resist leaving their comfort zones.

3. Fear of Alienation

The fear of wealth can be rooted in concerns about alienation from friends and family. Individuals may worry that financial success will strain relationships or lead to envy and resentment from loved ones.

4. Fear of Losing It All

For some, the fear of wealth revolves around the possibility of losing everything they've worked hard to accumulate. This fear can result in an overly cautious approach to investments or an aversion to taking calculated risks.

The Consequences of the Fear of Wealth

1. Self-Sabotage

The fear of wealth can lead to self-sabotage, where individuals unconsciously undermine their financial success through procrastination, poor investment decisions, or avoidance of wealth-building opportunities.

2. Missed Opportunities

Fearing wealth can cause individuals to miss out on valuable opportunities for personal and financial growth. It may prevent them from pursuing higher-paying careers, investing in their education, or taking calculated risks that could lead to financial success.

3. Reduced Life Satisfaction

Avoiding wealth due to fear can result in a lower quality of life than one's potential. It may limit access to experiences, resources, and opportunities that could enhance overall well-being.

Addressing and Overcoming the Fear of Wealth

1. Self-Reflection

Engage in self-reflection to identify the specific fears and anxieties you associate with wealth. Understanding the root causes of your fear is the first step in addressing it.

2. Financial Education

Invest in financial education and literacy to build confidence in handling wealth-related matters. The more you know about managing finances, the less daunting wealth becomes.

3. Seek Support

Consider seeking support from a financial advisor, therapist, or coach who specializes in wealth psychology. Professional guidance can help you navigate and address your fears more effectively.

4. Gradual Exposure

Take gradual steps towards wealth-building to acclimatize yourself to the responsibilities and changes that come with it. This can help ease the fear of sudden, overwhelming shifts in your life.

5. Open Communication

Maintain open and honest communication with loved ones about your financial goals and concerns. Addressing potential sources of alienation and envy can foster understanding and support within your social circle.

Embracing Wealth with Confidence

The fear of wealth need not limit your financial potential and life satisfaction. By acknowledging and addressing your fears, seeking support, and gradually acclimating to wealth-related responsibilities, you can embrace financial success with confidence and pave the way for a more fulfilling life.

In the chapters ahead, we will continue to explore the psychology of wealth and provide guidance on achieving financial success while nurturing a positive and empowered relationship with wealth.

Chapter 14

Money and Self-Worth

The intricate relationship between money and self-worth. Your sense of self-worth, or how you value and perceive yourself, can significantly impact your financial decisions, behaviors, and overall well-being. In this chapter, we'll explore this connection, its implications, and strategies for nurturing a healthy self-worth in your financial journey.

The Interplay of Money and Self-Worth

1. External Validation

Many people tie their self-worth to external markers of success, including their income, possessions, and financial achievements. The pursuit of these markers can lead to a fragile self-worth, as they are subject to change and external judgments.

2. Self-Worth and Financial Choices

Your self-worth can influence your financial choices. If you equate your net worth with your self-worth, financial setbacks or challenges may lead to feelings of inadequacy or failure.

3. The Myth of "Enough"

The constant pursuit of more wealth can be fueled by a belief that accumulating money will validate your self-worth. However, this pursuit often leads to a never-ending cycle of seeking external validation through material possessions.

The Implications of Tying Self-Worth to Money

1. Financial Anxiety

Linking self-worth to financial success can result in chronic financial anxiety. The fear of losing wealth or not meeting societal standards can lead to stress and emotional turmoil.

2. Relationships and Money

Relationships may be affected when self-worth is tied to money. Financial conflicts with partners, friends, or family members can escalate if your self-esteem is closely linked to your financial status.

3. Achievement Pressure

The pressure to constantly achieve financial milestones can be overwhelming. This constant drive for validation through wealth can hinder your ability to enjoy the present moment and find contentment.

Nurturing a Healthy Self-Worth in Your Financial Journey

1. Self-Reflection

Begin by engaging in self-reflection to explore your beliefs about self-worth and money. Recognize any negative or limiting beliefs and consider their origins.

2. Separate Self-Worth from Net Worth

Shift your perspective by consciously separating your self-worth from your financial status. Understand that your true value as a person is not determined by your bank balance.

3. Cultivate Self-Compassion

Practice self-compassion by treating yourself with the same kindness and understanding you would offer a friend. Embrace your imperfections and recognize that everyone faces financial challenges at some point.

4. Set Intrinsic Goals

Shift your focus from extrinsic goals, such as wealth and possessions, to intrinsic goals related to personal growth, relationships, and well-being. These goals can provide a more enduring source of self-worth.

5. Seek Support

Consider seeking support from a therapist or counselor if you struggle with deeply ingrained beliefs tying self-worth to money. Professional guidance can be transformative in reshaping these beliefs.

Embracing a Balanced Perspective

Money and self-worth are intertwined but distinct aspects of your life. By nurturing a healthy self-worth independent of your financial status, you can approach money with greater clarity, make more empowered financial decisions, and experience a more fulfilling and balanced life.

In the chapters ahead, we will continue to explore the psychology of wealth and provide guidance on achieving financial success while nurturing your self-worth and well-being.

Chapter 15

Managing Financial Stress

The critical topic of managing financial stress. Money-related worries and anxieties are common, but they need not control your life or undermine your well-being. In this chapter, we'll explore the causes of financial stress, its impact on your life, and practical strategies to effectively manage and reduce it.

Understanding Financial Stress

1. Common Stressors

Financial stress can stem from various sources, including debt, job loss, insufficient savings, unexpected expenses, or ongoing financial uncertainty. These stressors can create a sense of instability and anxiety.

2. Impact on mental and Physical Health

Financial stress can take a toll on both your mental and physical health. It may lead to symptoms of anxiety, depression, sleep disturbances, and even physical health issues like hypertension and heart disease.

3. Strain on Relationships

Financial stress can strain relationships with partners, family members, and friends. It often becomes a source of conflict, and communication breakdowns can further exacerbate stress.

Strategies for Managing Financial Stress

1. Financial Education

Invest in financial education to boost your confidence and understanding of money management. Knowledge can alleviate stress by empowering you to make informed financial decisions.

2. Budgeting and Planning

Create a realistic budget to gain control over your finances. Budgeting helps you track expenses, identify areas for savings, and plan for both short-term and long-term financial goals.

3. Emergency Fund

Build an emergency fund to provide a financial safety net during unexpected events. Having savings in place can reduce anxiety and stress associated with financial emergencies.

4. Seek Professional Advice

Consider consulting a financial advisor or counselor who specializes in helping individuals manage financial stress. They can provide personalized guidance and strategies for your unique situation.

5. Stress-Reduction Techniques

Incorporate stress-reduction techniques into your daily routine. Practices like mindfulness, meditation, deep breathing, or yoga can help you manage anxiety related to financial concerns.

6. Open Communication

Maintain open and honest communication with loved ones about your financial situation and concerns. Sharing your worries can foster understanding and support within your social circle.

7. Break Down Goals

Divide long-term financial goals into smaller, manageable steps. Achieving smaller milestones can boost your confidence and reduce the stress associated with large, daunting objectives.

8. Professional Development

Invest in your skills and education to enhance your career prospects. Professional growth can lead to increased job security and income, alleviating financial stress.

9. Debt Management

Develop a plan to manage and reduce debt systematically. Tackling debt can provide a sense of control and reduce financial stress over time.

10. Seek Support

If financial stress is significantly impacting your mental health, consider seeking support from a therapist or counselor. They can help you develop coping strategies and address the emotional aspects of financial stress.

Conclusion

Managing financial stress is crucial for your overall well-being and financial success. By implementing these strategies and seeking support when needed, you can effectively reduce the burden of financial stress and regain control over your financial life.

In the chapters ahead, we will continue to explore the psychology of wealth and provide guidance on achieving financial success while nurturing your mental and emotional health.

Chapter 16

Wealth Visualization Techniques

The powerful practice of wealth visualization. Visualization is a technique that harnesses the power of your imagination to manifest your financial goals and dreams. In this chapter, we'll delve into the art of wealth visualization, its benefits, and practical techniques to help you create a vivid and inspiring financial vision for your life.

The Power of Visualization

1. Imagining Your Financial Future

Visualization is the process of mentally picturing and experiencing your desired financial future. It involves creating a mental movie of your financial goals, allowing you to immerse yourself in the experience.

2. Enhancing Motivation

Visualization can boost your motivation by making your financial goals feel more attainable and real. When you vividly picture your success, you are more likely to stay committed to your wealth-building journey.

3. Reducing Anxiety

Visualization can help alleviate financial anxiety by shifting your focus from worries about the present to a positive vision of the future. It can calm your mind and reduce stress related to money.

Practical Wealth Visualization Techniques

1. Create a Vision Board

Design a vision board by collecting images, words, and symbols that represent your financial goals and aspirations. Display your vision board where you can see it daily, reinforcing your commitment to your wealth vision.

2. Guided Meditation

Engage in guided meditation sessions that focus on financial abundance and success. Many meditation apps and websites offer wealth-specific guided meditations to help you visualize your financial goals.

3. Visualization Journal

Maintain a visualization journal where you write down detailed descriptions of your financial goals and the emotions associated with achieving them. Regularly revisit and update your journal to reinforce your wealth vision.

4. Visualization Rituals

Incorporate visualization into your daily routine. Set aside dedicated time each day to vividly imagine yourself accomplishing your financial goals, feeling the emotions of success, and experiencing the benefits.

5. Positive Affirmations

Combine positive affirmations with visualization. Repeating affirmations related to financial success while visualizing your goals can reinforce your beliefs and bolster your confidence.

6. Role Models

Study the lives of successful individuals who have achieved financial abundance. Visualize yourself emulating their habits, making similar choices, and ultimately reaching your own financial success.

7. Visualization Partners

Share your wealth visualization journey with a friend or partner. Discuss your goals, support each other's visions, and hold one another accountable for staying committed to your financial dreams.

Maintaining a Wealth Visualization Practice

1. Consistency

Consistency is key to the effectiveness of wealth visualization. Make it a daily or weekly practice to keep your financial vision alive and vibrant in your mind.

2. Flexibility

Be open to adjusting your wealth visualization as your goals evolve. Life circumstances change, and your vision may need to adapt accordingly.

3. Patience

Remember that wealth visualization is a long-term practice. It may take time for your visions to manifest in reality, so be patient and persistent in your efforts.

Conclusion

Wealth visualization is a valuable tool for turning your financial aspirations into reality. By regularly immersing yourself in the experience of achieving your financial goals, you can boost motivation, reduce anxiety, and stay committed to your wealth-building journey.

In the chapters ahead, we will continue to explore the psychology of wealth and provide guidance on achieving financial success while nurturing your mental and emotional well-being.

Chapter 17

The Power of Positive Affirmations

The transformative practice of positive affirmations. Affirmations are simple yet potent statements that can reshape your mindset, boost your confidence, and manifest your financial goals. In this chapter, we'll delve into the art of positive affirmations, their benefits, and practical techniques to harness their power for wealth and abundance.

Unleashing the Potential of Positive Affirmations

1. What Are Positive Affirmations?

Positive affirmations are short, positive statements that you repeat to yourself regularly. They are designed to challenge and replace negative thoughts, beliefs, and self-doubt with empowering and uplifting messages.

2. The Mind-Body Connection

Affirmations work by tapping into the mind-body connection. When you repeatedly affirm positive beliefs, your subconscious mind begins to accept and internalize them, influencing your thoughts, feelings, and behaviors.

3. Transforming Limiting Beliefs

Affirmations can help you identify and transform limiting beliefs about money, wealth, and success. By replacing these beliefs with positive affirmations, you can shift your mindset toward abundance and opportunity.

Practical Techniques for Using Positive Affirmations

1. Identify Your Money Beliefs

Begin by identifying any negative or limiting beliefs you hold about money. Common examples include "money is the root of all evil" or "I will never be wealthy." Awareness is the first step to transformation.

2. Craft Empowering Affirmations

Create positive affirmations that directly challenge your identified limiting beliefs. For example, if you struggle with the belief that "money is scarce," an affirmation like "I attract abundance effortlessly" can counteract it.

3. Keep Them Specific and Personal

Make your affirmations specific and personal to your goals. Instead of a general statement like "I am successful," use one that aligns with your wealth aspirations, such as "I am building a successful and thriving financial future."

4. Repeat Regularly

Consistency is crucial. Repeat your affirmations daily, preferably in the morning and before bedtime. Repetition reinforces their impact on your subconscious mind.

5. Visualization and Emotion

Accompany your affirmations with visualization and emotion. As you recite your affirmations, vividly imagine the associated scenarios and feel the positive emotions they evoke.

6. Positive Affirmation Cards

Create affirmation cards or notes that you can carry with you throughout the day. When you encounter them, take a moment to recite the affirmation and internalize its message.

7. Mirror Work

Practice mirror work by looking into your own eyes as you recite your affirmations. This enhances the connection between your affirmations and your self-esteem.

8. Affirmations for Specific Goals

Craft affirmations tailored to specific financial goals, such as debt reduction, saving for a down payment, or increasing your income. These targeted affirmations can provide focused motivation.

Maintaining a Positive Affirmation Practice

1. Patience and Persistence

Be patient with the process. Transformation takes time, and your subconscious mind may resist change initially. Persistently use affirmations, and you will begin to notice shifts in your thinking.

2. Self-Compassion

Practice self-compassion and self-acceptance throughout your affirmation journey. Avoid self-criticism if you experience moments of doubt or skepticism.

3. Track Progress

Keep a journal to track your progress. Record any shifts in your thoughts, feelings, or behaviors related to money and wealth. Celebrate your successes along the way.

Conclusion

Positive affirmations are a potent tool for rewiring your mindset and manifesting your financial aspirations. By consistently applying these techniques, you can challenge limiting beliefs, boost your confidence, and create a positive relationship with money and wealth.

In the chapters ahead, we will continue to explore the psychology of wealth and provide guidance on achieving financial success while nurturing your mental and emotional well-being.

Chapter 18

The Psychology of Saving

Saving money is not just a practical financial habit; it's deeply intertwined with your thoughts, emotions, and behaviors. In this chapter, we'll explore the psychology behind saving, its challenges, and effective strategies to build a robust saving mindset.

The Psychology Behind Saving

1. Delayed Gratification

Saving involves delaying immediate consumption or spending in favor of future financial security or goals. It requires self-discipline and the ability to forgo short-term pleasures for long-term benefits.

2. Financial Security

The act of saving provides a sense of financial security and peace of mind. Knowing that you have a financial cushion can alleviate stress and anxiety related to unexpected expenses or emergencies.

3. Goal Achievement

Saving is often tied to specific financial goals, such as buying a home, starting a business, or retiring comfortably. The anticipation of achieving these goals can be a powerful motivator.

The Challenges of Saving

1. Instant Gratification

In a world of instant gratification, saving for the future can be challenging. The allure of immediate rewards from spending can overshadow the long-term benefits of saving.

2. Psychological Barriers

Psychological barriers, such as the fear of scarcity or a belief that one can't save, can hinder the saving process. Overcoming these barriers is essential for building a saving mindset.

3. Lifestyle Inflation

As income increases, some individuals succumb to lifestyle inflation, where their expenses rise in proportion to their earnings. This can make it difficult to save consistently.

Strategies for Building a Saving Mindset

1. Set Clear Goals

Define specific and achievable financial goals that give purpose to your saving efforts. Having a clear target provides motivation and direction.

2. Automate Savings

Automate your savings by setting up automatic transfers to a savings account or retirement fund. This ensures that saving becomes a non-negotiable part of your financial routine.

3. Pay Yourself First

Treat saving as an essential expense and prioritize it when allocating your income. Paying yourself first means saving a portion of your income before covering other expenses.

4. Create a Budget

Establish a budget to track your income and expenses. A budget helps you identify areas where you can cut back on spending and allocate more toward saving.

5. Emergency Fund

Build an emergency fund to cover unexpected expenses or financial setbacks. Having this financial safety net reduces the temptation to dip into your savings for emergencies.

6. Visualize Your Goals

Regularly visualize the achievement of your financial goals. The mental image of success can reinforce your commitment to saving.

7. Reward Yourself

Celebrate your saving milestones with small rewards or treats. Acknowledging your progress can boost your motivation to continue saving.

8. Review and Adjust

Periodically review your saving goals and financial situation. Adjust your goals and saving strategies as needed to stay aligned with your evolving financial priorities.

The Psychological Rewards of Saving

1. Peace of Mind

Saving provides peace of mind, knowing that you have financial resources to fall back on in times of need.

2. Financial Freedom

Accumulating savings gives you greater control over your financial future. It enables you to make choices based on your values and goals rather than financial necessity.

3. Confidence and Empowerment

A strong saving habit can boost your confidence and sense of empowerment. It demonstrates your ability to manage money effectively and achieve your financial aspirations.

Conclusion

The psychology of saving goes beyond simple money management; it's about understanding your motivations, overcoming challenges, and nurturing a mindset that supports your financial well-being.

By implementing the strategies discussed in this chapter and embracing the psychological rewards of saving, you can cultivate a strong saving mindset that empowers you to achieve your financial goals and secure your future.

In the chapters ahead, we will continue to explore the psychology of wealth and provide guidance on achieving financial success while nurturing your mental and emotional well-being.

Chapter 19

The Emotional Impact of Debt

The complex and often challenging topic of the emotional impact of debt. Debt can be more than just a financial burden; it can also take a toll on your emotions, well-being, and overall quality of life. In this chapter, we'll explore the emotional dimensions of debt, their consequences, and strategies to cope with and overcome the emotional challenges it presents.

The Emotional Dimensions of Debt

1. Stress and Anxiety

Debt often leads to heightened stress and anxiety. The constant worry about meeting payment deadlines, managing interest rates, and dealing with collection agencies can take a significant emotional toll.

2. Shame and Guilt

Many individuals burdened by debt experience feelings of shame and guilt. They may blame themselves for their financial predicament, even if external factors contributed to it.

3. Depression and Hopelessness

Debt can trigger or exacerbate feelings of depression and hopelessness. The weight of financial obligations and the perceived inability to escape debt can lead to a sense of despair.

4. Strain on Relationships

Debt-related stress can strain relationships with partners, family members, and friends. Conflicts over money and differing attitudes toward debt can escalate, causing emotional rifts.

Consequences of Debt-Related Emotional Distress

1. Impaired Mental Health

The emotional impact of debt can have a profound effect on mental health, leading to conditions such as anxiety disorders, depression, and even suicidal thoughts in extreme cases.

2. Physical Health Implications

Stress and anxiety related to debt can manifest physically, resulting in symptoms like insomnia, headaches, gastrointestinal problems, and cardiovascular issues.

3. Impact on Decision-Making

Emotional distress from debt can impair decision-making. Individuals may make impulsive or irrational financial choices in an attempt to alleviate emotional discomfort.

4. Reduced Quality of Life

The emotional burden of debt can diminish one's overall quality of life. It may restrict opportunities for enjoyment, limit social activities, and hinder personal and professional growth.

Coping Strategies for Dealing with Debt-Related Emotional Distress

1. Open Communication

Discuss your debt-related stress and emotions with trusted friends, family members, or a therapist. Sharing your feelings can provide emotional support and perspective.

2. Seek Professional Help

Consider seeking professional help from a therapist or counselor specializing in financial and emotional issues. They can help you develop coping strategies and address underlying emotional challenges.

3. Financial Planning

Work with a financial advisor to create a structured debt repayment plan. Having a clear strategy and timeline for debt reduction can alleviate anxiety and uncertainty.

4. Budgeting and Tracking Expenses

Establish a budget to track your income and expenses. A budget can help you regain control over your finances and reduce anxiety about managing money.

5. Mindfulness and Stress-Reduction Techniques

Practice mindfulness, meditation, or stress-reduction techniques to manage emotional distress. These practices can help you stay grounded and reduce the impact of anxiety.

6. Self-Compassion

Practice self-compassion by reframing your thoughts about debt. Recognize that financial challenges are common, and be kind to yourself as you work toward resolution.

7. Debt Support Groups

Consider joining a debt support group or online community. Sharing experiences and strategies with others facing similar challenges can provide a sense of belonging and motivation.

The Path to Emotional Healing and Debt Recovery

Dealing with the emotional impact of debt is a crucial aspect of the debt recovery process. By addressing and managing the emotional distress associated with debt, you can make informed financial decisions, regain control over your life, and work toward a future free from the emotional burdens of indebtedness.

In the chapters ahead, we will continue to explore the psychology of wealth and provide guidance on achieving financial success while nurturing your mental and emotional well-being.

Chapter 20

Financial Decision-Making Strategies

Where we'll explore a range of effective financial decision-making strategies. Making sound financial choices is essential for achieving your goals and securing your financial well-being. In this chapter, we'll delve into various strategies that can help you navigate complex financial decisions with confidence and wisdom.

The Importance of Informed Decision-Making

1. Financial Impact

Every financial decision you make has consequences that can affect your current and future financial well-being. Informed decisions can lead to better outcomes and greater financial security.

2. Reducing Stress

Informed decision-making can reduce financial stress by minimizing the uncertainty and anxiety often associated with financial choices.

3. Goal Achievement

Well-informed decisions are aligned with your financial goals, bringing you closer to achieving them efficiently.

Practical Financial Decision-Making Strategies

1. Set Clear Objectives

Begin by defining your financial objectives. Whether it's saving for retirement, buying a home, or paying off debt, having clear goals provides direction for your decisions.

2. Gather Information

Collect all relevant information before making a decision. This may include financial data, market research, or advice from experts.

3. Assess Risks and Benefits

Evaluate the potential risks and benefits of each option. Consider both short-term and long-term implications to make well-rounded assessments.

4. Consider Opportunity Cost

Think about the opportunity cost of your decision. What are you giving up by choosing one option over another? Assess the trade-offs involved.

5. Create a Pros and Cons List

Compile a list of pros and cons for each option. This visual aid can clarify your thinking and highlight the most advantageous choice.

6. Seek Professional Advice

Consult financial advisors or experts when necessary. Their knowledge and expertise can provide valuable insights and guidance for complex financial decisions.

7. Sleep on It

Take your time with important financial decisions. Avoid making hasty choices by giving yourself time to reflect and consider the consequences.

8. Embrace a Systematic Approach

Develop a systematic decision-making process. This could involve gathering information, evaluating options, seeking advice, and then making an informed choice.

Emotional Aspects of Financial Decision-Making

1. Emotional Awareness**

Recognize the emotional aspects of financial decisions. Emotions can influence choices, so being aware of them is crucial for making rational decisions.

2. Manage Stress

Implement stress-management techniques when facing major financial decisions. Stress can cloud judgment, so keeping it in check is essential.

3. Avoid Impulse Decisions

Resist the urge to make impulsive decisions based solely on emotions. Take a step back and apply rational thinking.

Review and Adjust

1. Monitor Outcomes

After making a financial decision, regularly review its outcomes. Assess whether the choice aligns with your goals and make adjustments if necessary.

2. Learn from Experience

Use past financial decisions as learning experiences. Recognize what worked well and what didn't and apply those lessons to future decisions.

3. Flexibility

Be flexible in your approach to financial decision-making. Life circumstances change, so your strategies may need to adapt accordingly.

Conclusion

Sound financial decision-making is an essential skill for achieving your financial aspirations and maintaining financial well-being. By employing the strategies discussed in this chapter, you can approach financial choices with greater confidence, minimize stress, and ensure that your decisions align with your goals.

In the chapters ahead, we will continue to explore the psychology of wealth and provide guidance on achieving financial success while nurturing your mental and emotional well-being.

Chapter 21

Setting and Achieving Financial Goals

The art of setting and achieving financial goals. Your financial journey is shaped by the goals you set and the steps you take to reach them. In this chapter, we'll explore the importance of setting financial goals, the process of goal setting, and strategies to help you turn your aspirations into tangible accomplishments.

The Significance of Financial Goals

1. Vision and Purpose

Financial goals provide you with a vision and purpose for your financial life. They give meaning to your financial decisions and actions.

2. Motivation and Focus

Having clear financial goals can boost your motivation and keep you focused on your desired outcomes. They serve as a reminder of what you're working toward.

3. Progress Measurement

Financial goals act as benchmarks to measure your progress. They help you track your achievements and make adjustments as needed.

The Process of Setting Financial Goals

1. Self-Reflection

Begin by reflecting on your financial values, aspirations, and priorities. What truly matters to you in terms of financial success?

2. Define Specific Goals

Translate your reflections into specific, measurable, achievable, relevant, and time-bound (SMART) financial goals. For example, instead of "save more money," specify "save $10,000 for a down payment on a home by December 31, 20XX."

3. Prioritize Goals

Not all financial goals are equally important or urgent. Prioritize your goals based on their significance and your current financial situation.

4. Break Down Goals

Divide large or long-term goals into smaller, more manageable milestones. This approach makes the path to achieving your goals feel less overwhelming.

5. Create an Action Plan

Develop a clear action Plan outlining the steps you need to take to achieve each goal. Assign responsibilities and deadlines where necessary.

6. Review and Adjust

Regularly review your goals and progress. Be open to adjusting your goals and action plans as your circumstances change or new opportunities arise.

Strategies for Achieving Financial Goals

1. Automate Savings

Set up automatic transfers to your savings or investment accounts to ensure consistent progress toward your goals.

2. Budgeting

Create a budget that allocates funds specifically for your financial goals. This helps you track your progress and avoid overspending.

3. Emergency Fund

Prioritize building an emergency fund as one of your first financial goals. Having this safety net can protect your other financial aspirations from unexpected setbacks.

4. Debt Reduction

If you have debt, consider debt reduction as a goal. Paying down high-interest debt can free up more resources for other goals.

5. Financial Education

Invest in financial education to improve your knowledge and decision-making skills. Understanding financial concepts can help you make more informed choices.

6. Seek Professional Advice

Consult with financial advisors or experts when necessary. They can provide guidance and strategies to help you achieve complex financial goals.

7. Visualize Success

Regularly visualize yourself achieving your financial goals. This mental imagery can boost motivation and reinforce your commitment.

Celebrate Your Achievements

Remember to celebrate your achievements along the way. Acknowledging your progress and successes can keep you motivated and inspired to continue pursuing your financial goals.

Conclusion

Setting and achieving financial goals is a dynamic and empowering process that propels you toward a more secure and fulfilling financial future. By following the steps and strategies outlined in this chapter, you can define your financial aspirations, create a roadmap for success, and enjoy the satisfaction of turning your dreams into reality.

In the chapters ahead, we will continue to explore the psychology of wealth and provide guidance on achieving financial success while nurturing your mental and emotional well-being.

Chapter 22

Wealth and Generosity

The harmonious relationship between wealth and generosity. While wealth often brings financial security and comfort, it's through acts of generosity that we can truly enrich our lives and those of others. In this chapter, we'll delve into the significance of generosity, its benefits, and practical ways to incorporate it into your financial journey.

The Significance of Generosity

1. Beyond Material Wealth

Generosity extends beyond monetary giving; it encompasses the willingness to share your time, talents, and resources with others. It reflects a spirit of abundance and a desire to make a positive impact.

2. Emotional Fulfillment

Acts of generosity often lead to a deep sense of fulfillment and happiness. Giving can create meaningful connections, foster gratitude, and enhance overall well-being.

3. Strengthening Relationships

Generosity can strengthen personal and social relationships. It builds trust, fosters empathy, and promotes a sense of unity within communities and families.

The Benefits of Generosity

1. Improved Mental Health

Generosity has been linked to improved mental health, reducing stress, anxiety, and symptoms of depression. It can provide a sense of purpose and satisfaction.

2. Enhanced Physical Health

Acts of kindness and generosity have been associated with lower blood pressure, reduced inflammation, and overall better physical health.

3. Increased Happiness

Generosity often leads to increased happiness and life satisfaction. The act of giving can trigger the brain's reward system, generating feelings of joy.

Practical Ways to Incorporate Generosity

1. Charitable Giving

Donate to causes or organizations that align with your values and passions. Regularly contribute a portion of your wealth to support initiatives that matter to you.

2. Volunteering

Offer your time and skills as a volunteer for local charities, nonprofits, or community events. Volunteering allows you to make a direct and hands-on impact.

3. Random Acts of Kindness

Engage in random acts of kindness, such as paying for someone's meal, helping a stranger in need, or leaving encouraging notes for others.

4. Philanthropic Planning

Consider philanthropic planning as part of your financial strategy. Establish a charitable foundation or trust to support causes you're passionate about in a structured and sustainable manner.

5. Mentorship and Education

Share your knowledge and expertise with others through mentorship or educational programs. Guiding someone on their financial journey can be a transformative form of generosity.

6. Family Giving Tradition

Foster a culture of giving within your family. Encourage discussions about generosity, involve family members in charitable decisions, and initiate family philanthropic projects.

The Ripple Effect of Generosity

1. Inspiring Others

Your acts of generosity can inspire others to do the same, creating a ripple effect of kindness and positive change.

2. Collective Impact

When individuals and communities come together through acts of generosity, they can address societal issues and bring about significant change.

3. Personal Growth

Generosity can lead to personal growth by broadening your perspective, deepening empathy, and fostering a sense of purpose.

Conclusion

Generosity is a powerful force that not only benefits those on the receiving end but also enriches the lives of givers. As you continue your financial journey, consider how you can incorporate generosity into your wealth-building strategy.

By embracing a spirit of abundance and actively seeking opportunities to give, you can create a fulfilling and impactful relationship between wealth and generosity.

In the chapters ahead, we will continue to explore the psychology of wealth and provide guidance on achieving financial success while nurturing your mental, emotional, and social well-being.

Chapter 23

The Psychology of Investments

The captivating world of the psychology of investments. Investing is not just about numbers and market trends; it's equally influenced by your thoughts, emotions, and behavioral patterns. In this chapter, we'll explore the psychological aspects of investing, common biases that affect decisions, and strategies to make informed and emotionally intelligent investment choices.

Understanding the Psychology of Investments

1. Risk and Reward

Investing inherently involves risk and the potential for reward. Your willingness to tolerate risk and your perception of it play a crucial role in investment decisions.

2. Emotions and Biases

Emotions like fear, greed, and overconfidence can cloud judgment and lead to impulsive or irrational investment choices. Recognizing and managing these emotions is essential.

3. Long-Term Perspective

Investing often requires a long-term perspective. The ability to resist short-term market fluctuations and stay focused on your financial goals is a psychological challenge.

Common Psychological Biases in Investing

1. Confirmation Bias

Investors tend to seek information that confirms their existing beliefs and ignore contrary evidence. This bias can lead to overconfidence and poor decision-making.

2. Loss Aversion

Many investors fear losses more than they value gains. This bias can lead to a reluctance to sell losing investments, even when it's financially prudent.

3. Herd Mentality

Following the crowd is a common tendency. Herd mentality can lead to excessive buying during market booms and panic selling during downturns.

4. Overconfidence

Overestimating your knowledge and abilities as an investor can lead to taking on too much risk or making speculative investments.

5. Anchoring

Investors often anchor their decisions to a specific reference point, such as the purchase price of a stock. This can lead to holding onto an investment for emotional rather than rational reasons.

Strategies for Emotionally Intelligent Investing

1. Education and Research

Invest in financial education and research to enhance your understanding of investment concepts and markets. Knowledge can boost confidence and reduce emotional decision-making.

2. Diversification

Diversify your investment portfolio across different asset classes to spread risk. Diversification can provide a sense of security and reduce the emotional impact of individual investments.

3. Investment Plan

Create a well-thought-out investment plan with clear goals, risk tolerance, and a long-term perspective. Having a plan can help you stay disciplined during market fluctuations.

4. Regular Review

Periodically review and rebalance your investment portfolio to ensure it aligns with your goals and risk tolerance. Avoid making impulsive changes based on short-term market movements.

5. Seek Professional Guidance

Consider consulting with a financial advisor or investment professional for personalized guidance and to help counteract emotional biases.

6. Practice Patience

Cultivate patience as an investor. Avoid the temptation to react impulsively to market volatility, and maintain your focus on long-term objectives.

7. Emotional Awareness

Develop self-awareness regarding your emotions and biases in investment decisions. Regularly assess your emotional state and its potential impact on your choices.

The Intersection of Psychology and Investing

1. Behavioral Finance

Behavioral finance is an emerging field that combines psychology and economics to understand and explain investor behavior and market anomalies.

2. Emotional Intelligence

Emotional intelligence is a valuable trait for investors. It involves recognizing and managing your own emotions while also understanding the emotions of others in the market.

Conclusion

The psychology of investments is a fascinating and essential aspect of successful wealth management.

By understanding your own psychological biases, developing emotional intelligence, and implementing the strategies outlined in this chapter, you can make informed and emotionally intelligent investment choices.

In the chapters ahead, we will continue to explore the psychology of wealth and provide guidance on achieving financial success while nurturing your mental and emotional well-being.

Chapter 24

Money and Relationships

The intricate connection between money and relationships. Money can be a significant source of both joy and stress in our lives, particularly within the context of our closest relationships. In this chapter, we'll explore the dynamics of money in relationships, common challenges it poses, and strategies to navigate financial matters harmoniously with your loved ones.

The Role of Money in Relationships

1. Communication and Trust

Open and honest communication about money fosters trust and understanding within relationships. It's a crucial component of a healthy financial partnership.

2. Shared Goals

Aligning financial goals with your partner promotes unity and a sense of shared purpose. Working toward common objectives can strengthen your bond.

3. Conflict and Stress

Financial conflicts can lead to stress, arguments, and relationship strain. How you handle these conflicts can significantly impact the quality of your relationship.

Common Challenges in Money and Relationships

1. Different Financial Values

Individuals often have different mindsets and values. These differences can lead to misunderstandings and conflicts.

2. Income Disparities

Income disparities within a relationship can create power imbalances and emotional tensions. It's essential to address these disparities openly and constructively.

3. Hidden Financial Issues

Concealing financial problems or debts can erode trust and lead to major relationship breakdowns.

4. Financial Planning

The absence of a clear financial plan can result in disorganization and a lack of direction, leading to stress and uncertainty.

Strategies for Navigating Money in Relationships

1. Open and Honest Communication

Create a safe space for open and honest conversations about money. Share your financial goals, values, and concerns with your partner.

2. Establish Shared Goals

Work together to establish shared financial goals that reflect both your individual aspirations and your joint objectives as a couple or family.

3. Budgeting Together

Collaborate on creating a joint budget that outlines how you'll manage expenses, save, and allocate resources.

4. Regular Financial Check-In

Schedule regular financial check-ins to review your financial progress and make adjustments as needed. This practice can help prevent misunderstandings.

5. Seek Professional Help

If financial conflicts persist, consider seeking the assistance of a financial therapist or counselor who specializes in money and relationships.

6. Set Boundaries

Discuss and establish boundaries regarding financial independence and personal spending. Agree on limits for individual discretionary expenses.

7. Address Debt Together

If one or both partners have debt, develop a plan to address it together. Work as a team to reduce and manage debt effectively.

8. Plan for the Future

Discuss and plan for long-term financial goals, such as retirement, homeownership, or children's education. Ensure you're on the same page about your future aspirations.

9. Shared Responsibilitie

Determine how you'll share financial responsibilities, including bill payment, savings contributions, and investment decisions.

The Value of Money in Relationships

1. Strengthened Bond

When managed thoughtfully, money can strengthen the bond between partners by fostering trust, cooperation, and shared experiences.

2. Mutual Growth

Money can be a tool for mutual growth and achievement, allowing couples to support each other in realizing their dreams.

3. Lifelong Learning

Navigating money together offers opportunities for lifelong learning and personal development, both individually and as a couple.

Conclusion

Money and relationships are deeply intertwined, and how you manage financial matters can profoundly impact the harmony and satisfaction within your partnerships.

By practicing open communication, setting shared goals, and addressing financial challenges together, you can build a solid foundation for a healthy and prosperous financial relationship.

In the chapters ahead, we will continue to explore the psychology of wealth and provide guidance on achieving financial success while nurturing your mental, emotional, and social well-being.

Chapter 25

Financial Communication in Couples

The vital topic of financial communication in couples. Money is often cited as one of the leading causes of conflict in relationships. However, by developing effective communication strategies, couples can navigate financial discussions with greater ease, strengthen their partnership, and work together towards their financial goals.

The Importance of Financial Communication

1. Building Trust

Open and honest financial communication is the foundation of trust in a relationship. It fosters transparency and understanding between partners.

2. Goal Alignment

Discussing finances helps ensure that both partners are on the same page regarding their financial goals and aspirations. It paves the way for setting shared objectives.

3. Conflict Resolution

Effective financial communication is essential for resolving conflicts related to money. It allows couples to address differences constructively.

Effective Financial Communication Strategies

1. Set a Regular Meeting Time

Designate a specific time for financial discussions, ensuring that both partners are present and focused.

2. Be Honest and Open

Encourage open and honest conversations about your financial situation, including income, expenses, debts, and goals.

3. Use "I" Statements

Frame your statements using "I" rather than "you" to express your feelings and concerns without assigning blame. For example, say, "I feel anxious about our financial situation" instead of "You're spending too much."

4. Active Listening

Practice active listening by giving your full attention when your partner is speaking. Avoid interrupting or planning your response while they talk.

5. Be Empathetic

Acknowledge and validate your partner's feelings and perspectives, even if they differ from your own. Empathy can bridge gaps in understanding.

6. Set Shared Goals

Work together to set clear financial goals that reflect both individual and joint aspirations. Discuss how you'll achieve these objectives as a team.

7. Create a Joint Budget

Collaborate on creating a joint budget that outlines your income, expenses, savings, and investments. Ensure that both partners have input and agree on the budget.

8. Allocate Responsibilities

Determine how you'll divide financial responsibilities, such as bill payment, saving contributions, and investment decisions. Establishing roles can reduce misunderstandings.

9. Emergency Plan

Develop a financial emergency plan outlining what steps to take in case of unexpected expenses or income disruptions.

10. Address Debt Together

If one or both partners have debt, discuss a strategy for managing and reducing it as a team.

11. Seek Professional Guidance

Consider consulting with a financial advisor or therapist specializing in financial issues for couples. Professional guidance can be invaluable for resolving complex financial matters.

12. Celebrate Milestone

Celebrate financial milestones and achievements as a couple. Recognizing your progress can strengthen your sense of partnership and shared accomplishment.

The Benefits of Effective Financial Communication

1. Strengthened Bond

Effective financial communication strengthens the bond between partners by promoting trust, empathy, and understanding.

2. Conflict Resolution

Couples who communicate well about money can address conflicts constructively, reducing tension and stress in the relationship.

3. Shared Vision

Financial discussions help couples create a shared vision for their future, fostering alignment and a sense of purpose.

Conclusion

Financial communication is a skill that can be developed and refined over time.

By embracing open, honest, and empathetic conversations about money, couples can build a solid foundation for their financial partnership, strengthen their relationship, and work together towards their shared financial goals.

In the chapters ahead, we will continue to explore the psychology of wealth and provide guidance on achieving financial success while nurturing your mental, emotional, and social well-being within the context of your relationships.

Chapter 26

The Psychological Impact of Windfalls

The fascinating world of windfalls and their profound psychological impact. Windfalls, unexpected financial gains or inheritances, have the potential to bring both joy and challenges. In this chapter, we'll delve into the psychological dimensions of windfalls, how they affect our emotions and behaviors, and strategies to navigate them wisely.

Understanding Windfalls

1. Types of Windfalls

Windfalls can take various forms, including lottery winnings, inheritances, unexpected bonuses, and even surprise financial gifts.

2. Emotional Complexity

Receiving a windfall often triggers a range of emotions, from excitement and gratitude to anxiety and guilt.

3. Life-Changing Potential

Windfalls have the potential to transform lives, providing financial security, opportunities for growth, and the ability to pursue dreams.

The Psychological Impact of Windfalls

1. Emotional Rollercoaster

The initial emotional response to a windfall is often euphoria and excitement. However, this can be followed by anxiety, stress, and even guilt as the reality of managing the windfall sets in.

2. Lifestyle Inflation

Some individuals experience lifestyle inflation, where they rapidly increase their spending and adopt a more extravagant lifestyle, which can lead to financial instability.

3. Family Dynamics

Windfalls can also affect family dynamics, sometimes leading to tension and disputes over how to handle the newfound wealth.

Strategies for Navigating Windfalls

1. Pause and Reflect

Take time to pause and reflect on the windfall before making any major decisions. Avoid impulsive spending or investment choices.

2. Seek Professional Guidance

Consult with financial advisors and professionals who can help you develop a comprehensive plan for managing the windfall wisely.

3. Set Clear Goals

Define clear financial goals and objectives for the windfall. Consider short-term needs, long-term aspirations, and philanthropic endeavors.

4. Budget and Plan

Create a detailed budget and financial plan that outlines how you'll use the windfall to achieve your goals while maintaining financial stability.

5. Address Debt and Savings

Prioritize paying off high-interest debt and establishing or bolstering your emergency fund. These steps provide a solid financial foundation.

6. Diversify Investments

If you choose to invest a portion of the windfall, diversify your investments to spread risk and align with your financial goals.

7. Philanthropy and Giving Back

Consider allocating a portion of the windfall to philanthropic endeavors or charitable contributions. Giving back can be emotionally rewarding and provide a sense of purpose.

8. Communicate with Family

If the windfall impacts your family, communicate openly and honestly with family members about your plans and expectations.

9. Manage Expectations

Manage your own and others' expectations about the windfall. It's important to set realistic and sustainable financial goals.

The Long-Term Perspective

1. Sustainable Wealth

Approach the windfall with a long-term perspective, focusing on building sustainable wealth and financial security for the future.

2. Emotional Well-being

Recognize that the psychological impact of a windfall can be ongoing. Continue to nurture your emotional well-being as you navigate the changes it brings.

3. Seek Emotional Support

If you find that the psychological impact of the windfall is challenging to manage, consider seeking emotional support from a therapist or counselor.

Conclusion

Windfalls can be transformative, offering opportunities and challenges that extend beyond the financial realm.

By understanding and managing the psychological impact of windfalls with prudence and emotional intelligence, you can use this unexpected wealth to create a brighter financial future while nurturing your mental and emotional well-being.

In the chapters ahead, we will continue to explore the psychology of wealth and provide guidance on achieving financial success while maintaining a healthy and balanced life.

Chapter 27

Financial Independence

We'll embark on a journey toward financial independence. Financial independence, often referred to as FI, is a goal that many aspire to achieve. It signifies the ability to sustain your desired lifestyle without relying solely on employment income. In this chapter, we'll explore what financial independence entails, why it's valuable, and practical steps to work towards this liberating goal.

Defining Financial Independence

1. Freedom of Choice

Financial independence provides you with the freedom to make choices based on your values and desires rather than financial constraints.

2. Lifelong Securit

Achieving financial independence offers lifelong security, ensuring that you can meet your needs and aspirations, even in retirement.

3. Reduced Stress

It significantly reduces financial stress, allowing you to focus on your well-being, personal growth, and the pursuit of your passions.

The Path to Financial Independence

1. Determine Your FI Number

Calculate your FI number—the amount of savings and investments required to support your desired lifestyle without relying on employment income.

2. Develop a Financial Plan

Create a comprehensive financial plan that outlines your income, expenses, savings, and investment strategies to achieve your FI number.

3. Emergency Fund

Prioritize building and maintaining an emergency fund to cover unexpected expenses and provide financial stability.

4. Debt Management

Address and reduce high-interest debt, as it can hinder your progress toward financial independence.

5. Invest Wisely

Invest your savings strategically in a diversified portfolio to grow your wealth and generate passive income.

6. Save Aggressively

Increase your savings rate by living below your means and consistently funneling surplus income into your savings and investments.

7. Multiple Income Streams

Explore opportunities for multiple income streams, such as side hustles, rental income, or passive investments, to accelerate your journey.

8. Minimize Expenses

Regularly review your expenses and look for areas where you can cut costs without sacrificing your quality of life.

9. Tax Efficiency

Optimize your tax strategy to minimize tax liabilities and retain more of your income.

The Benefits of Financial Independence

1. Peace of Mind

Financial independence brings peace of mind, reducing anxiety about financial stability in the face of unexpected events.

2. Enhanced Lifestyle Choices

It empowers you to make lifestyle choices based on your preferences rather than financial constraints.

3. Pursue Passion Projects

Financial independence enables you to pursue passion projects, hobbies, or creative endeavors without worrying about financial pressures.

4. Retirement Freedom

Achieving financial independence early in life allows for early retirement or the option to work on your own terms.

5. Generosity

It provides the capacity to be more generous and support causes you care about through philanthropy and charitable contributions.

The Importance of Patience

1. Long-Term Perspective

Financial independence often requires a long-term perspective. It may take years of disciplined saving and investing to reach your FI number.

2. Lifestyle Moderation

Moderation in your lifestyle choices during the journey to financial independence can expedite your progress.

3. Adjust as Needed

Be flexible and adjust your financial plan as circumstances change. Life events and financial markets can impact your path.

Conclusion

Financial independence is not just about accumulating wealth; it's about gaining control over your financial destiny and embracing a life that aligns with your values and aspirations.

By setting clear goals, managing your finances wisely, and maintaining patience and discipline, you can embark on the path to financial independence.

In the chapters ahead, we will continue to explore the psychology of wealth and provide guidance on achieving financial success while nurturing your mental, emotional, and social well-being within the context of financial independence.

Chapter 28

Wealth and Health

The intricate connection between wealth and health. While financial prosperity can enhance various aspects of your life, it's essential to recognize the profound impact wealth can have on your physical and mental well-being. In this chapter, we'll delve into the multifaceted relationship between wealth and health, why it matters, and strategies for achieving a harmonious balance between the two.

The Interplay Between Wealth and Health

1. Financial Security

Financial stability and access to quality healthcare services can enhance your physical health by providing timely medical care and preventive measures.

2. Stress and Health

Excessive financial stress can have detrimental effects on your mental and physical health, including increased risk of anxiety, depression, and chronic illnesses.

3. Lifestyle Choices

Financial well-being can influence lifestyle choices, such as nutrition, exercise, and access to leisure activities, which in turn impact your overall health.

The Impact of Wealth on Health

1. Access to Healthcare

Wealth often provides better access to healthcare facilities, specialists, and medical treatments, resulting in improved health outcomes.

2. Reduced Stress

Financial stability can reduce stress levels, positively impact mental health and reducing the risk of stress-related illnesses.

3. Healthier Lifestyle

Having the means to afford a balanced diet, exercise equipment or memberships, and wellness programs can promote a healthier lifestyle.

4. Quality of Life

Financial prosperity can enhance your overall quality of life, leading to increased happiness and life satisfaction, which are linked to better health.

The Role of Health in Wealth

1. Productivity

Good health is a critical factor in maintaining productivity and achieving career success, which can contribute to increased wealth.

2. Longevity

Improved health can lead to a longer life expectancy, allowing you more time to accumulate wealth and enjoy the benefits of your financial success.

3. Healthcare Costs

Good health can help control healthcare costs, preventing excessive expenses that may erode your wealth.

Strategies for Balancing Wealth and Health

1. Prioritize Health

Recognize the importance of health as a fundamental component of your overall well-being. Prioritize regular exercise, a balanced diet, and preventive healthcare.

2. Stress Management

Develop effective stress management techniques, such as mindfulness, meditation, or relaxation exercises, to mitigate the impact of financial stress on your health.

3. Financial Planning

Engage in comprehensive financial planning that includes saving for healthcare costs, insurance coverage, and retirement planning to secure your financial future.

4. Work-Life Balance

Strive for a healthy work-life balance to prevent burnout and prioritize self-care, leisure, and time spent with loved ones.

5. Seek Professional Help

Consult with healthcare professionals and financial advisors when needed to make informed decisions about your health and finances.

6. Philanthropy

Consider philanthropy as a way to support causes related to health and well-being, allowing you to use your wealth for positive social impact.

Conclusion

Wealth and health are intricately intertwined aspects of a fulfilling and prosperous life.

By recognizing the symbiotic relationship between the two and proactively managing both, you can enjoy the benefits of financial success while nurturing your physical and mental well-being.

In the chapters ahead, we will continue to explore the psychology of wealth and provide guidance on achieving financial success while maintaining a healthy and balanced life.

Chapter 29

The Role of Patience in Wealth Building

The invaluable role of patience in the journey of wealth building. Building wealth is a long-term endeavor that requires not only financial discipline but also the ability to embrace delayed gratification. In this chapter, we'll delve into the significance of patience, how it influences your financial success, and strategies to cultivate and harness the power of patience in your wealth-building journey.

The Significance of Patience

1. Long-Term Perspective

Patience is the ability to maintain a long-term perspective on your financial goals, resisting the temptation for immediate rewards.

2. Delayed Gratification

It involves delaying immediate desires or spending in favor of saving and investing for future financial security and prosperity.

3. Emotional Resilience

Patience fosters emotional resilience, helping you navigate market volatility, setbacks, and financial challenges without making impulsive decisions.

Patience and Wealth Building

1. Compound Interest

Patience allows you to leverage the power of compound interest, where your money earns interest on both the principal and previously earned interest.

2. Strategic Investing

Long-term investors who exercise patience can ride out market fluctuations, benefiting from the market's historical upward trajectory.

3. Wealth Accumulation

Patience is a fundamental driver of wealth accumulation, enabling you to steadily save, invest, and grow your wealth over time.

4. Risk Mitigation

By avoiding impulsive decisions, you can mitigate risks associated with speculative investments or hasty financial choices.

Cultivating Patience

1. Set Clear Goals

Define clear and achievable financial goals that provide a sense of purpose and direction, anchoring your patience.

2. Create a Financial Plan

Develop a comprehensive financial plan that outlines your savings, investment strategies, and timelines for achieving your goals.

3. Embrace Mindfulness

Practice mindfulness to remain present and avoid becoming overly focused on future financial rewards. This can help you stay patient.

4. Diversify Investments

Diversify your investment portfolio to spread risk and reduce the emotional impact of individual investments' fluctuations.

5. Educate Yourself

Invest in financial education to better understand investment principles, market cycles, and the benefits of patience.

6. Seek Professional Advice

Consult with financial advisors who can provide guidance, reassurance, and perspective during challenging financial times.

7. Develop Emotional Intelligence

Strengthen your emotional intelligence to manage the anxiety, fear, or impatience that may arise during your wealth-building journey.

The Rewards of Patience

1. Financial Security

Patience leads to financial security, providing a safety net for unexpected expenses and retirement.

2. Emotional Well-being

It contributes to emotional well-being by reducing financial stress and anxiety, enhancing overall life satisfaction.

3. Confidence

Patience instills confidence in your financial decisions, empowering you to stay the course, even during challenging times.

Conclusion

Patience is an indispensable virtue in the pursuit of wealth building. By understanding its significance, cultivating it through mindfulness and education, and implementing patient strategies in your financial plan, you can harness the power of patience to achieve lasting financial success.

In the chapters ahead, we will continue to explore the psychology of wealth and provide guidance on achieving financial success while nurturing your mental, emotional, and social well-being.

Chapter 30

Money and Work-Life Balance

The delicate balance between money and work-life harmony. Money is often a driving force behind our careers, but it's essential to strike a balance that allows you to enjoy financial success without sacrificing your well-being, relationships, and personal fulfillment. In this chapter, we'll delve into the relationship between money and work-life balance, why it matters, and strategies to achieve a fulfilling equilibrium.

The Nexus of Money and Work-Life Balance

1. Career Pursuits

Money can be a significant motivator for career choices and professional ambitions, potentially leading to imbalances in work and personal life.

2. Financial Security

Achieving financial security can reduce the pressure to overwork and enable you to make career decisions aligned with your values.

3. Time vs. Money

Balancing the pursuit of money with time spent on personal interests, relationships, and leisure is essential for overall life satisfaction.

The Impact of Money on Work-Life Balance

1. Overwork

The desire for financial success can lead to overwork, causing burnout, stress, and strained personal relationships.

2. Prioritization

Money often necessitates trade-offs between work and personal life, requiring conscious choices about how you allocate your time.

3. Career Satisfaction

Balancing money and work-life is essential for career satisfaction, as excessive focus on income may overshadow personal fulfillment.

Strategies for Achieving Work-Life Balance

1. Define Your Values

Identify your core values and priorities in both your career and personal life to guide your decisions and actions.

2. Financial Planning

Create a comprehensive financial plan that aligns with your goals, providing financial security and peace of mind.

3. Set Boundaries

Establish clear boundaries between work and personal life to protect your time for relaxation, hobbies, and relationships.

4. Time Management

Prioritize time management to optimize productivity during work hours, allowing for quality personal time outside of work.

5. Embrace Flexibility

Explore flexible work arrangements or freelancing opportunities that offer greater control over your work schedule.

6. Regular Evaluations

Regularly assess your work-life balance to ensure that your priorities and values align with your actions.

7. Seek Support

Seek support from mentors, colleagues, or counselors to help you navigate career choices and work-life challenges.

The Rewards of Work-Life Balance

1. Improved Well-being

Balancing money and work-life leads to improved physical and mental well-being, reducing stress and promoting overall health.

2. Stronger Relationships

It nurtures healthier personal relationships by allowing you to spend quality time with loved ones and foster deeper connections.

3. Career Fulfillment

Achieving work-life balance contributes to career satisfaction by enabling you to pursue roles and opportunities that resonate with your values.

4. Personal Growth

It fosters personal growth and self-discovery, providing time and energy for hobbies, passions, and personal development.

Conclusion

Balancing money and work-life is a dynamic and ongoing process that requires self-awareness, prioritization, and conscious choices. By defining your values, creating a financial plan that aligns with your goals, and implementing strategies to protect your work-life harmony, you can enjoy the benefits of financial success while nurturing your overall well-being.

In the chapters ahead, we will continue to explore the psychology of wealth and provide guidance on achieving financial success while maintaining a balanced and fulfilling life.

Chapter 31

Wealth and Risk-Taking

The intricate relationship between wealth and risk-taking. Wealth accumulation often involves navigating various forms of risk, from financial investments to entrepreneurial endeavors. In this chapter, we'll delve into the dynamic interplay between wealth and risk, how it influences financial success, and strategies for making informed and calculated risks a part of your wealth-building journey.

The Role of Risk in Wealth Building

1. Calculated Ventures

Wealth building often requires embracing calculated risks, where potential rewards outweigh potential losses.

2. Investment Decisions

Risk plays a crucial role in investment decisions, influencing the types of assets you choose and the potential returns on your investments.

3. Entrepreneurship

Entrepreneurs frequently take calculated risks to create and grow businesses, which can lead to substantial wealth if successful.

The Impact of Risk on Wealth

1. Growth Potential

Taking calculated risks can lead to higher investment returns, business profitability, and wealth accumulation.

2. Volatility

Risks can introduce volatility into your financial journey, requiring patience and adaptability to navigate market fluctuations.

3. Mitigation Strategies

Successful wealth builders often employ risk mitigation strategies to protect their assets and financial security.

Strategies for Managing Risk in Wealth Building

1. Diversification

Diversify your investments to spread risk and reduce the impact of losses in any single asset or market.

2. Risk Assessment

Conduct thorough risk assessments before making financial decisions, evaluating potential rewards and losses.

3. Risk Tolerance

Understand your risk tolerance, which influences your willingness to accept uncertainty and potential loss in pursuit of financial goals.

4. Financial Planning

Incorporate risk management into your financial plan, setting aside emergency funds and insurance coverage to protect against unexpected setbacks.

5. Professional Advice

Seek guidance from financial advisors or experts who can provide insights and strategies for managing risk effectively.

6. Education

Invest in financial education to enhance your understanding of risk, investment principles, and market dynamics.

7. Monitor and Adjust

Regularly monitor your investments and financial plan, adjusting your strategies as needed to adapt to changing market conditions.

The Rewards of Calculated Risk-Taking

1. Wealth Accumulation

Calculated risk-taking can lead to significant wealth accumulation through successful investments or entrepreneurial ventures.

2. Financial Growth

It can accelerate financial growth and allow you to achieve your financial goals more quickly than conservative strategies.

3. Confidence

Embracing risk can boost your confidence in financial decision-making and your ability to navigate challenges.

Conclusion

Risk-taking is an inherent part of the wealth-building journey, and when approached thoughtfully and strategically, it can be a powerful tool for achieving financial success.

By understanding your risk tolerance, implementing risk management strategies, and seeking professional guidance, you can harness the potential rewards of calculated risk-taking while safeguarding your financial security.

In the chapters ahead, we will continue to explore the psychology of wealth and provide guidance on achieving financial success while maintaining a balanced and fulfilling life.

Chapter 32

The Psychology of Entrepreneurship

The fascinating world of entrepreneurship and explore the intricate psychology behind it. Entrepreneurship is not just about starting and running businesses; it's a mindset, a way of thinking and approaching challenges. In this chapter, we'll delve into the psychology of entrepreneurship, examining the traits, mindset, and strategies that can lead to entrepreneurial success.

The Entrepreneurial Mindset

1. Visionary Thinking

Entrepreneurs often possess a visionary mindset, the ability to see opportunities where others see obstacles and to envision innovative solutions.

2. Risk-Taking

Entrepreneurship involves calculated risk-taking, the willingness to step into the unknown and embrace uncertainty for the sake of potential rewards.

3. Adaptability

Successful entrepreneurs are adaptable and flexible, capable of pivoting their strategies in response to changing circumstances.

4. Resilience

Resilience is a hallmark of entrepreneurship. Entrepreneurs bounce back from setbacks, learning and growing from failures.

Psychological Traits of Entrepreneurs

1. Passion and Drive

Entrepreneurs are often driven by a deep passion for their vision, giving them the determination to overcome obstacles.

2. Independence

Entrepreneurs value independence and autonomy, seeking to create their path rather than following traditional career paths.

3. Creativity

Creative thinking is a cornerstone of entrepreneurship, allowing for the development of innovative products, services, and solutions.

4. Self-Confidence

Entrepreneurs possess self-confidence in their abilities and vision, which can inspire others to join their journey.

Challenges and Psychological Resilience

1. Uncertainty

The entrepreneurial journey is rife with uncertainty, requiring resilience and the ability to manage stress and anxiety.

2. Failure

Failure is a common aspect of entrepreneurship, and the ability to bounce back from it is a testament to an entrepreneur's psychological strength.

3. Loneliness

Entrepreneurs may experience loneliness due to the isolation of decision-making and leadership. Building a support network is crucial.

Strategies for Developing Entrepreneurial Psychology

1. Mindfulness

Practice mindfulness to stay present and reduce anxiety about the future. Being in the moment can improve decision-making.

2. Continuous Learning

Foster a commitment to lifelong learning, staying updated on industry trends and seeking personal growth opportunities.

3. Resilience Training

Engage in resilience training to develop strategies for coping with setbacks and stressors that come with entrepreneurship.

4. Networking

Build a strong support network by networking with fellow entrepreneurs, mentors, and advisors who can provide guidance and encouragement.

5. Seek Feedback

Seek feedback from customers, peers, and mentors to refine your ideas and strategies.

The Rewards of Entrepreneurship

1. Personal Fulfillment

Entrepreneurship offers the potential for personal fulfillment, as you bring your vision to life and make a positive impact on your industry or community.

2. Financial Rewards

Successful entrepreneurship can lead to significant financial rewards, providing financial security and wealth-building opportunities.

3. Independence

Entrepreneurs enjoy independence and the ability to make decisions that align with their values and goals.

4. Legacy Building

Entrepreneurship allows for the creation of a legacy, leaving a mark on the world through innovative solutions and ventures.

Conclusion

The psychology of entrepreneurship is a captivating journey filled with opportunities for growth, personal fulfillment, and financial success.

By understanding the entrepreneurial mindset, nurturing the necessary traits, and developing strategies for resilience and adaptability, you can embark on your entrepreneurial path with confidence and enthusiasm.

In the chapters ahead, we will continue to explore the psychology of wealth and provide guidance on achieving financial success while maintaining a balanced and fulfilling life, whether through entrepreneurship or other avenues.

Chapter 33

Wealth and Education

The profound relationship between wealth and education. Education is not only a means of personal development but also a powerful tool for wealth accumulation and financial success. In this chapter, we'll delve into how education influences wealth, the various paths to educational attainment, and strategies for leveraging education to enhance your financial well-being.

The Intersection of Education and Wealth

1. Education as an Investment

Education is often regarded as one of the most valuable investments you can make in yourself, with the potential for significant long-term returns.

2. Potential Income

Higher levels of education are generally associated with increased income potential and greater earning capacity over a lifetime.

3. Financial Literacy

Education equips individuals with financial literacy, enabling them to make informed decisions about money management, investments, and financial planning.

The Impact of Education on Wealth

1. Income Growth

Education can lead to higher-paying job opportunities and career advancement, resulting in increased income and wealth accumulation.

2. Financial Stability

Well-educated individuals are better equipped to manage their finances, build savings, and maintain financial stability.

3. Entrepreneurship

Education fosters entrepreneurial skills and knowledge, increasing the likelihood of success for those pursuing business ventures.

4. Investment Savvy

Educated individuals are more likely to engage in strategic investments and wealth-building strategies.

Paths to Educational Attainment

1. Traditional Education

Traditional education includes primary, secondary, and tertiary levels, culminating in degrees or certifications from schools, colleges, and universities.

2. Online Learning

Online learning has become increasingly accessible, allowing individuals to pursue education at their own pace through virtual courses and programs.

3. Vocational Training

Vocational training and trade schools offer specialized education for careers in skilled trades, providing a path to financial success.

4. Self-Education

Self-education involves a commitment to continuous learning through books, online resources, and mentorship.

Strategies for Leveraging Education for Wealth

1. Set Educational Goals

Define clear educational goals that align with your career aspirations and financial objectives.

2. Financial Planning

Incorporate education-related expenses into your financial plan, considering tuition, materials, and potential student loans.

3. Scholarships and Grants

Explore opportunities for scholarships, grants, and financial aid to reduce the financial burden of education.

4. Lifelong Learning

Cultivate a habit of lifelong learning, continually seeking opportunities to enhance your knowledge and skills.

5. Networking

Leverage educational institutions and networks to connect with like-minded individuals, mentors, and potential collaborators.

6. Apply Knowledge

Apply the knowledge and skills gained through education to advance your career, build wealth, and make informed financial decisions.

The Rewards of Educational Investment

1. Career Advancement

Education opens doors to career advancement, leading to higher-paying and more fulfilling job opportunities.

2. Financial Security

Well-educated individuals often enjoy greater financial security, with the ability to build savings and withstand economic challenges.

3. Entrepreneurial Success

Education equips aspiring entrepreneurs with the knowledge and skills to launch and manage successful ventures.

4. Personal Growth

Education fosters personal growth, enhancing critical thinking, problem-solving, and adaptability.

Conclusion

Education is a powerful catalyst for wealth accumulation and personal development.

By recognizing the value of education, setting clear educational goals, and investing in your knowledge and skills, you can unlock the potential for greater financial success and a more fulfilling life.

In the chapters ahead, we will continue to explore the psychology of wealth and provide guidance on achieving financial success while maintaining a balanced and fulfilling life, fueled by the power of education.

Chapter 34

The Emotional Cost of Impulse Buying

The emotional consequences of impulse buying and its impact on your overall well-being. Impulse buying refers to the act of making unplanned purchases, often driven by immediate desires or emotions. While it can provide momentary satisfaction, it can also come at an emotional cost. In this chapter, we'll delve into the psychological aspects of impulse buying, the emotions it can trigger, and strategies for regaining control over your spending habits.

The Psychology of Impulse Buying

1. Immediate Gratification

Impulse buying is driven by the desire for immediate gratification, as individuals seek to satisfy their wants or emotions in the moment.

2. Emotional Triggers

Emotions such as boredom, stress, excitement, or sadness can trigger impulsive spending as individuals attempt to regulate their feelings.

3. Marketing Influence

Marketers often use persuasive techniques to capitalize on impulsive tendencies, creating a sense of urgency or excitement.

The Emotional Consequences

1. Buyer's Remorse

Impulse purchases can lead to buyer's remorse, a feeling of regret and guilt after realizing the unnecessary expenditure.

2. Financial Stress

Frequent impulse buying can lead to financial stress as it erodes your savings and budget.

3. Emotional Rollercoaster

Impulse buying can create an emotional rollercoaster, with moments of euphoria followed by disappointment and stress.

4. Decluttering Frustration

Accumulating unnecessary items can lead to clutter and frustration, adding to emotional distress.

Strategies for Regaining Control

1. Pause and Reflect

When tempted to make an impulse purchase, pause and reflect on whether it aligns with your financial goals and needs.

2. Create a Budget

Establish a budget that allocates a specific amount for discretionary spending, helping you make conscious choices.

3. List and Prioritize

Create a list of items you genuinely need or want and prioritize them, focusing on essentials before indulgences.

4. Delay Gratification

Practice delayed gratification by waiting for a predetermined period before making non-essential purchases.

5. Emotional Awareness

Develop emotional awareness by identifying your triggers for impulse buying and seeking alternative ways to manage emotions.

6. Unsubscribe and Unfollow

Remove shopping apps, unsubscribe from promotional emails, and unfollow retail brands on social media to reduce exposure to temptations.

7. Accountability Partner

Share your financial goals with a trusted friend or family member who can hold you accountable for your spending habits.

The Emotional Rewards of Mindful Spending

1. Peace of Mind

Mindful spending brings peace of mind, knowing that your financial decisions align with your goals and values.

2. Reduced Stress

It reduces financial stress and allows you to maintain better control over your finances.

3. Improved Well-being

Mindful spending can lead to improved emotional well-being and a sense of empowerment over your financial future.

Conclusion

Impulse buying may offer temporary gratification, but it often comes at an emotional cost that can undermine your overall well-being. By understanding the psychology of impulse buying, recognizing its emotional consequences, and implementing mindful spending strategies, you can regain control over your financial habits and experience the emotional rewards of responsible and intentional consumption. In the chapters ahead, we will continue to explore the psychology of wealth and provide guidance on achieving financial success while nurturing your mental, emotional, and social well-being.

Chapter 35

Wealth and Retirement Planning

We'll embark on a journey into the world of retirement planning and explore how it intersects with your wealth. Retirement is a significant milestone in life, and careful planning is essential to ensure financial security and a fulfilling retirement lifestyle. In this chapter, we'll delve into the importance of retirement planning, strategies for building a retirement nest egg, and tips for making the most of your golden years.

The Significance of Retirement Planning

1. Financial Security

Retirement planning is about securing your financial future, ensuring that you have the means to enjoy a comfortable and stress-free retirement.

2. Lifestyle Choices

It allows you to make informed decisions about your retirement lifestyle, from travel and hobbies to healthcare and leisure activities.

3. Peace of Mind

Effective retirement planning provides peace of mind, reducing anxiety about financial stability during your retirement years.

Building Your Retirement Nest Egg

1. Start Early

Begin saving for retirement as early as possible to take advantage of compound interest and maximize your savings.

2. Set Clear Goals

Define your retirement goals, including your desired retirement age, lifestyle, and financial needs.

3. Diversify Investments

Diversify your retirement portfolio to spread risk and ensure a balanced mix of assets.

4. Maximize Contributions

Contribute regularly to retirement accounts such as 401(k)s, IRAs, or employer-sponsored plans to make the most of tax benefits and employer matching.

5. Seek Professional Advice

Consult with financial advisors who specialize in retirement planning to create a personalized retirement strategy.

Navigating Retirement Transitions

1. Transition Planning

Plan for the transition into retirement by considering how you'll replace your work-related income.

2. Healthcare Coverage

Ensure you have adequate healthcare coverage in retirement, including Medicare or private health insurance.

3. Social Security

Understand the benefits of Social Security and the best time to start receiving them based on your financial needs.

4. Estate Planning

Create or update your estate plan, including wills, trusts, and powers of attorney, to protect your assets and wishes.

Making the Most of Retirement

1. Pursue Passions

Use retirement as an opportunity to pursue passions, hobbies, and interests that you may not have had time for during your working years.

2. Stay Active

Engage in regular physical and mental activities to maintain your health and vitality in retirement.

3. Give Back

Consider volunteering or charitable activities to stay connected with your community and give back.

4. Financial Monitoring

Continuously monitor your retirement finances to ensure your savings last throughout your retirement.

5. Adjust as Needed

Be open to adjusting your retirement plans as circumstances change, including financial markets and health.

The Rewards of Effective Retirement Planning

1. Financial Freedom

Effective retirement planning provides financial freedom, allowing you to enjoy retirement without financial worries.

2. Peaceful Retirement

It fosters a peaceful and stress-free retirement, where you can focus on the things you love.

3. Legacy and Generosity

Retirement planning enables you to leave a legacy for loved ones or support charitable causes.

4. Fulfillment

A well-planned retirement can lead to a fulfilling and purpose-driven life in your later years.

Conclusion

Retirement planning is a vital component of your financial journey, ensuring that you can enjoy your retirement years to the fullest.

By starting early, setting clear goals, seeking professional guidance, and staying adaptable, you can achieve financial security and the freedom to embrace the retirement lifestyle you've envisioned.

In the chapters ahead, we will continue to explore the psychology of wealth and provide guidance on achieving financial success while maintaining a balanced and fulfilling life, both before and during retirement.

Chapter 36

Overcoming Scarcity Mindset

We'll delve into the concept of scarcity mindset and explore strategies for overcoming it. Scarcity mindset is a belief system rooted in the fear of limited resources, leading to feelings of lack and insecurity. It can affect various aspects of your life, including your finances, relationships, and overall well-being. In this chapter, we'll examine the psychology of scarcity mindset, its impact, and techniques to shift your mindset towards abundance and fulfillment.

Understanding Scarcity Mindset

1. Fear of Insufficiency

Scarcity mindset is characterized by a constant fear of insufficiency, where individuals believe there's not enough to go around.

2. Hoarding Mentality

It often leads to hoarding of resources, whether it's money, time, or opportunities, out of fear that they might disappear.

3. Negative Self-Talk

Individuals with a scarcity mindset tend to engage in negative self-talk, doubting their abilities and potential for success.

4. Short-Term Focus

Scarcity mindset tends to prioritize short-term solutions over long-term planning due to the sense of urgency it creates.

The Impact of Scarcity Mindset

1. Financial Stress

Scarcity mindset can lead to chronic financial stress, as individuals worry about their ability to cover expenses and save for the future.

2. Relationship Strain

It can strain relationships, as the fear of scarcity may lead to conflicts over money and resources.

3. Missed Opportunities

A scarcity mindset can prevent individuals from seizing opportunities for personal and professional growth.

4. Reduced Well-being

Overall well-being can suffer, with individuals feeling trapped and unfulfilled due to a constant focus on what they lack.

Strategies for Overcoming Scarcity Mindset

1. Self-Awareness

Recognize when scarcity mindset is at play by identifying negative thought patterns and behaviors related to scarcity.

2. Mindfulness

Practice mindfulness to stay present and grounded, reducing anxiety about future scarcity.

3. Abundance of Affirmations

Replace negative self-talk with abundance affirmations that reinforce a mindset of plenty and gratitude.

4. Shift to Long-Term Thinking

Gradually shift your focus towards long-term planning and delayed gratification, understanding that resources can be cultivated over time.

5. Share and Collaborate

Embrace the power of sharing and collaboration, as working with others can often lead to more significant opportunities and resources.

6. Seek Education

Invest in financial and personal development education to improve your skills and knowledge, boosting your confidence and potential.

7. Financial Planning

Create a comprehensive financial plan that aligns with your goals and helps you build a sense of financial security.

The Rewards of an Abundance Mindset

1. Financial Freedom

Abundance mindset fosters financial freedom, allowing you to make informed financial decisions and investments.

2. Stronger Relationships

It nurtures healthier relationships as you become more open to collaboration and sharing with others.

3. Opportunity Magnet

An abundance mindset attracts opportunities and possibilities, as you become more receptive to new ventures and experiences.

4. Enhanced Well-being

Overall well-being improves as you shift your focus from scarcity to abundance, leading to a more fulfilling and joyful life.

Conclusion

Overcoming scarcity mindset is a transformative journey that can profoundly impact your financial success, relationships, and overall well-being.

By cultivating self-awareness, practicing mindfulness, and adopting strategies that promote abundance, you can break free from the constraints of scarcity and embrace a mindset that empowers you to live a more fulfilling and prosperous life.

In the chapters ahead, we will continue to explore the psychology of wealth and provide guidance on achieving financial success while nurturing your mental, emotional, and social well-being.

Chapter 37

Money and Social Comparison

The intriguing relationship between money and social comparison. Social comparison is a natural human tendency to assess ourselves in relation to others. When it comes to wealth and finances, this tendency can significantly impact our emotions, behaviors, and financial well-being. In this chapter, we'll explore the psychology of social comparison in the context of money, its effects, and strategies for managing these comparisons in a healthy and constructive way.

The Role of Social Comparison

1. Benchmarking

Social comparison serves as a benchmark for evaluating our own financial status, often by comparing ourselves to friends, family, colleagues, or even strangers.

2. Status and Identity

Money is frequently tied to our social identity, and social comparisons can influence our self-esteem and sense of belonging.

3. Lifestyle Expectations

Comparison can lead to lifestyle expectations, where individuals strive to maintain a certain image or standard based on what they perceive others have.

The Effects of Social Comparison on Money

1. Envy and Jealousy

Comparing ourselves to those with more wealth can trigger feelings of envy and jealousy, which can be emotionally taxing.

2. Anxiety and Stress

Social comparisons can lead to anxiety and stress as individuals worry about not measuring up to the financial success of others.

3. Unhealthy Spending Habits

Attempting to keep up with the Joneses can result in unhealthy spending habits, leading to financial instability and debt.

4. Decreased Satisfaction

Constant comparison can decrease overall life satisfaction, as the focus shifts away from personal values and contentment.

Strategies for Managing Social Comparison

1. Self-Reflection

Reflect on your values, goals, and priorities to establish a clear understanding of what financial success means to you.

2. Gratitude Practice

Cultivate gratitude by focusing on what you have rather than what you lack, fostering contentment and reducing envy.

3. Limit Exposure

Limit exposure to social media and other platforms that may promote unhealthy social comparisons.

4. Financial Planning

Develop a comprehensive financial plan that aligns with your goals and values, regardless of external comparisons.

5. Seek Support

Seek support from friends, family, or professionals who can provide guidance and a more balanced perspective.

6. Celebrate Achievements

Celebrate your financial achievements and milestones, no matter how small, to reinforce a sense of progress and accomplishment.

The Rewards of Healthy Social Comparison

1. Improved Financial Well-being

Healthy social comparison can inspire you to make positive financial changes and investments based on your own goals, rather than external pressures.

2. Reduced Stress

Managing social comparison can lead to reduced stress and anxiety, allowing you to focus on your personal financial journey.

3. Enhanced Relationships

It can foster stronger and more authentic relationships, as you become less preoccupied with superficial comparisons.

4. Increased Satisfaction

Embracing a healthier approach to social comparison can result in increased overall life satisfaction and contentment.

Conclusion

Money and social comparison often go hand in hand, influencing our emotions and financial behaviors.

By cultivating self-awareness, practicing gratitude, and developing strategies to manage social comparisons, you can regain control over your financial decisions and well-being. Embrace your unique financial journey, stay true to your values, and remember that your financial success is defined by your personal goals, not by how you stack up against others.

In the chapters ahead, we will continue to explore the psychology of wealth and provide guidance on achieving financial success while maintaining a balanced and fulfilling life, free from the constraints of unhealthy social comparisons.

Chapter 38

The Psychology of Giving Back

Where we'll explore the profound psychology behind giving back and the transformative impact it can have on both individuals and communities. Giving back, whether through charitable donations, volunteering, or acts of kindness, is a powerful way to connect with others, find purpose, and experience the joy of making a positive difference in the world. In this chapter, we'll delve into the psychology of giving, its benefits, and strategies for incorporating giving back into your life in a meaningful way.

The Motivation Behind Giving

1. Empathy and Compassion

Empathy and compassion are strong motivators for giving back, as they drive individuals to alleviate the suffering of others.

2. Altruism

Altruism, the selfless concern for the well-being of others, is a fundamental human trait that often fuels acts of giving.

3. Personal Fulfillment

Giving back can lead to personal fulfillment and a sense of purpose, enriching the lives of both givers and recipients.

The Benefits of Giving Back

1. Enhanced Well-being

Engaging in acts of generosity can boost overall well-being by promoting feelings of happiness, gratitude, and satisfaction.

2. Strengthened Relationships

Giving back can strengthen social bonds and relationships, as it fosters a sense of connection and shared values.

3. Stress Reduction

Acts of kindness and giving have been linked to stress reduction and improved mental health.

4. Sense of Belonging

Contributing to a cause or community can provide a sense of belonging and make you feel like you're part of something larger than yourself.

Strategies for Incorporating Giving into Your Life

1. Identify Your Passion

Identify causes or issues that resonate with your values and interests, ensuring that your giving aligns with your passions.

2. Set Clear Goals

Establish clear goals for your giving, whether it's a specific amount, time commitment, or impact you want to achieve.

3. Start Small

Begin with small acts of kindness and gradually increase your level of involvement as you become more comfortable with giving back.

4. Research and Vet Organizations

When donating money or time, research and vet organizations to ensure your contributions are used effectively and responsibly.

5. Involve Loved Ones

Involve friends or family in your giving efforts, creating shared experiences and values that strengthen relationships.

6. Volunteer Your Skills

Consider volunteering your skills and expertise to contribute to causes in a way that leverages your unique talents.

The Rewards of Giving Back

1. Fulfillment and Joy

Giving back provides a profound sense of fulfillment and joy that comes from knowing you've made a positive impact.

2. Connection and Community

It fosters connections with others who share your values, creating a sense of community and belonging.

3. Personal Growth

Giving back can lead to personal growth and a deeper understanding of the world and its challenges.

4. Legacy and Impact

Through giving back, you have the opportunity to leave a lasting legacy of positive change and impact.

Conclusion

The psychology of giving back is a testament to the innate human desire to connect, help others, and find purpose in making the world a better place.

By understanding the motivation behind giving, recognizing the benefits it offers, and implementing strategies to incorporate giving into your life, you can experience the profound rewards of contributing to the well-being of others and, in turn, enriching your own life.

In the chapters ahead, we will continue to explore the psychology of wealth and provide guidance on achieving financial success while nurturing your mental, emotional, and social well-being through acts of generosity and giving back.

Chapter 39

Financial Self-Care

Where we'll explore the concept of financial self-care and its importance in maintaining a healthy relationship with your finances. Just as you prioritize physical and mental well-being, financial self-care is a crucial aspect of your overall wellness. In this chapter, we'll delve into the psychology of financial self-care, its benefits, and practical strategies to integrate it into your life.

Understanding Financial Self-Care

1. Holistic Well-being

Financial self-care is an integral part of holistic well-being, recognizing the interplay between financial health and other aspects of your life.

2. Mindful Money Management

It involves mindful money management, fostering a positive and intentional approach to your financial decisions.

3. Stress Reduction

Financial self-care can reduce stress and anxiety related to money, contributing to better mental and emotional health.

4. Long-Term Goals

It aligns your financial behaviors with long-term goals, ensuring that your actions support your aspirations.

The Benefits of Financial Self-Care

1. Reduced Financial Stress

Engaging in financial self-care can lead to reduced financial stress, allowing you to focus on your well-being and goals.

2. Improved Financial Health

It contributes to improved financial health by promoting responsible spending, saving, and investing habits.

3. Enhanced Emotional Well-being

Financial self-care enhances emotional well-being, as you gain control over your financial situation and experience peace of mind.

4. Empowerment and Confidence

It empowers you to make informed financial decisions and fosters confidence in your ability to navigate financial challenges.

Strategies for Practicing Financial Self-Care

1. Budgeting and Planning

Create a realistic budget and financial plan that aligns with your goals, ensuring that you have a clear roadmap for your finances.

2. Regular Financial Check-ins

Schedule regular financial check-ins to review your progress, adjust your plan as needed, and celebrate your achievements.

3. Debt Management

Address and manage any existing debt by creating a plan for repayment and avoiding unnecessary debt accumulation.

4. Emergency Fund

Build an emergency fund to provide a financial safety net in case unexpected expenses arise.

5. Invest in Financial Education

Invest in your financial education by reading books, attending seminars, or seeking guidance from financial professionals.

6. Practice Delayed Gratification

Practice delayed gratification by resisting impulsive spending and focusing on long-term financial goals.

7. Seek Support

Don't hesitate to seek support from financial advisors, therapists, or support groups when dealing with financial challenges.

The Rewards of Financial Self-Care

1. Financial Freedom

Financial self-care leads to financial freedom, where you can make choices that align with your values and goals.

2. Improved Relationships

It can enhance your relationships by reducing financial stress and promoting open communication about money.

3. Peace of Mind

Financial self-care provides peace of mind, allowing you to face financial uncertainties with confidence.

4. Personal Growth

Engaging in financial self-care contributes to personal growth, as you develop resilience and financial competency.

Conclusion

Financial self-care is an essential component of your overall well-being, ensuring that you can enjoy a life free from the burden of financial stress and uncertainty.

By understanding the importance of financial self-care, recognizing its benefits, and implementing practical strategies, you can cultivate a positive and mindful relationship with your finances. In the chapters ahead, we will continue to explore the psychology of wealth and provide guidance on achieving financial success while nurturing your mental, emotional, and social well-being through thoughtful financial self-care practices.

Chapter 40

The Connection Between Mindfulness and Wealth

Where we'll explore the intriguing connection between mindfulness and wealth. Mindfulness, the practice of being fully present and aware in the moment, extends beyond personal well-being and has a profound impact on your financial success and overall wealth. In this chapter, we'll delve into the psychology of mindfulness, its influence on financial decisions, and strategies for integrating mindfulness into your financial journey.

Understanding Mindfulness

1. Present Moment Awareness

Mindfulness involves being fully present in the current moment, free from judgment and distractions.

2. Emotional Regulation

It helps you recognize and regulate your emotions, allowing you to make more rational and considered financial decisions.

3. Clarity and Focus

Mindfulness enhances clarity and focus, enabling you to set clear financial goals and make intentional choices.

4. Reduced Stress

Practicing mindfulness can reduce stress, which can improve overall decision-making and financial well-being.

The Impact of Mindfulness on Wealth

1. Improved Financial Decisions

Mindfulness cultivates better decision-making by promoting rationality and reducing impulsive behaviors.

2. Effective Goal Setting

It enhances the effectiveness of goal setting, allowing you to set and achieve financial objectives with greater success.

3. Reduced Emotional Spending

Mindfulness helps reduce emotional spending by promoting awareness of your triggers and providing healthier coping mechanisms.

4. Better Money Management

It fosters better money management skills, such as budgeting, saving, and investing, by promoting discipline and self-control.

Strategies for Integrating Mindfulness into Your Financial Journey

1. Mindful Budgeting

Practice mindful budgeting by regularly reviewing your expenses and income, making adjustments as needed to align with your financial goals.

2. Financial Goal Visualization

Visualize your financial goals with mindfulness techniques, reinforcing your commitment to achieving them.

3. Delayed Gratification

When faced with financial choices, practice delayed gratification by taking time to consider the long-term consequences of your decisions.

4. Mindful Spending

Before making purchases, employ mindfulness to assess whether they align with your values and financial priorities.

5. Emotional Awareness

Cultivate emotional awareness by identifying your emotional triggers related to money and seeking alternative ways to manage them.

6. Regular Meditation Practice

Incorporate regular meditation or mindfulness exercises into your routine to strengthen your mindfulness muscle.

The Rewards of Mindful Wealth

1. Enhanced Financial Success

Mindful wealth practices lead to enhanced financial success, as you make decisions that align with your values and goals.

2. Reduced Financial Stress

They reduce financial stress and anxiety, allowing you to navigate financial challenges with greater resilience.

3. Improved Well-being

Mindful wealth practices contribute to overall well-being, fostering a sense of contentment and balance in your life.

4. Sustainable Wealth

Mindfulness helps you build sustainable wealth by encouraging responsible financial habits and decision-making.

Conclusion

Mindfulness is a powerful tool that extends its benefits beyond personal well-being, directly impacting your financial success and wealth.

By embracing mindfulness, you can make more informed financial decisions, set and achieve your financial goals, and enjoy a more balanced and fulfilling relationship with money. In the chapters ahead, we will continue to explore the psychology of wealth and provide guidance on achieving financial success while nurturing your mental, emotional, and social well-being through the practice of mindfulness.

Chapter 41

The Impact of Social Media on Financial Well-being

The intriguing and complex relationship between social media and financial well-being. Social media has become an integral part of Modern life, influencing various aspects of our daily routines, including how we perceive and manage our finances. In this chapter, we'll delve into the psychology behind the impact of social media on financial well-being, the positive and negative effects, and strategies for maintaining a healthy financial mindset in the digital age.

The Influence of Social Media

1. Social Comparison

Social media platforms provide a constant stream of curated content that often leads to social comparison, where individuals compare their own financial situations to those of their peers.

2. Lifestyle Showcase

Many users showcase their lifestyles, possessions, and achievements, which can create unrealistic financial expectations.

3. Investment Advice

Social media is a source of investment advice and financial news, influencing investment decisions and risk tolerance.

4. Consumerism

The prevalence of advertisements and influencers can encourage consumerism and impulsive spending.

The Positive Impact

1. Financial Education

Social media offers access to financial education resources, empowering individuals to make informed decisions.

2. Investment Opportunities

It can provide insights into investment opportunities and financial trends, helping individuals diversify their portfolios.

3. Supportive Communities

Online communities and forums can offer support and advice for individuals facing financial challenges.

The Negative Impact

1. Unrealistic Expectations

Social media often presents an idealized version of reality, leading to unrealistic financial expectations and discontent.

2. Impulsive Spending

Constant exposure to advertisements and influencers can encourage impulsive spending and debt accumulation.

3. Financial Stress

Comparing oneself to others on social media can lead to financial stress and a sense of inadequacy.

4. Investment Risk

Following investment advice on social media can lead to increased investment risk and losses.

Strategies for Managing Social Media's Impact

1. Mindful Consumption

Practice mindful consumption of social media by being aware of its potential impact on your financial well-being.

2. Curate Your Feed

Curate your social media feed to include content that promotes financial education, positivity, and inspiration.

3. Set Boundaries

Set time limits and boundaries for social media usage to prevent overexposure and negative effects.

4. Financial Literacy

Invest in financial literacy by seeking out reputable sources of financial education and advice.

5. Evaluate Investment Advice

Before acting on investment advice from social media, conduct thorough research and consider consulting a financial professional.

6. Limit Impulse Buying

Practice restraint and avoid impulsive purchases influenced by social media content.

The Rewards of Mindful Social Media Usage

1. Improved Financial Well-being

Mindful social media usage can lead to improved financial well-being by reducing impulsive spending and financial stress.

2. Informed Decision-making

It promotes informed decision-making by encouraging individuals to seek reliable financial information.

3. Stronger Financial Mindset

Mindful consumption of social media fosters a stronger and more resilient financial mindset.

4. Reduced Comparison

It reduces the negative impact of social comparison, allowing individuals to focus on their unique financial journey.

Conclusion

Social media's impact on financial well-being is undeniable, but with mindfulness and informed usage, you can harness its benefits while minimizing its negative effects.

By curating your online experience, seeking financial education, and maintaining a balanced perspective, you can ensure that social media remains a valuable tool in your financial journey, rather than a hindrance.

In the chapters ahead, we will continue to explore the psychology of wealth and provide guidance on achieving financial success while nurturing your mental, emotional, and social well-being in today's digital age.

Chapter 42

Wealth and Identity

The complex and often multifaceted relationship between wealth and identity. Our identity, the way we perceive ourselves and how others perceive us, is influenced by various factors, and wealth is undeniably one of them. In this chapter, we'll explore the psychology behind how wealth can shape identity, the impact it has on individuals and society, and strategies for developing a healthy and authentic sense of self in the context of wealth.

The Interplay Between Wealth and Identity

1. Self-Perception

For many, their wealth, or lack thereof, plays a significant role in shaping their self-perception.

2. External Validation

Society often equates financial success with personal worth, leading individuals to seek external validation through wealth.

3. Social Status

Wealth can influence one's social status and the way they are perceived by others, contributing to their identity.

4. Values and Priorities

Individuals often align their values and priorities with their financial status, which can influence their identity.

The Impact of Wealth on Identity

1. Self-Worth

Wealth can influence feelings of self-worth, with some individuals associating their value with their financial success.

2. Identity Conflicts

For those with sudden wealth or significant financial changes, identity conflicts can arise as they navigate their new financial reality.

3. Social Comparisons

Constant social comparisons based on wealth can lead to identity crises and feelings of inadequacy.

4. Materialism

An emphasis on material possessions can distort one's identity, prioritizing materialism over personal growth and values.

Strategies for Developing Healthy Identity in the Context of Wealth

1. Self-Reflection

Engage in self-reflection to understand the role of wealth in your self-perception and identify values that truly matter to you.

2. Authenticity

Strive for authenticity by aligning your actions and decisions with your core values and identity, rather than external expectations.

3. Empathy and Perspective

Cultivate empathy and a broader perspective by acknowledging that wealth does not define a person's worth or identity.

4. Self-Validation

Practice self-validation, recognizing your intrinsic worth beyond your financial status.

5. Balance and Well-being

Prioritize balance and well-being in all aspects of life, fostering a sense of identity that extends beyond wealth.

6. Contribution and Legacy

Consider how you can use your wealth to contribute positively to society and leave a meaningful legacy.

The Rewards of a Healthy Identity in Wealth

1. Inner Fulfillment

Developing a healthy identity in the context of wealth leads to inner fulfillment and contentment.

2. Authentic Relationships

It fosters authentic and meaningful relationships based on shared values, rather than materialistic interests.

3. Resilience

A strong and authentic identity provides resilience in the face of financial challenges or changes.

4. Positive Impact

It allows you to make a positive impact on society and leave a legacy that extends beyond material wealth.

Conclusion

The relationship between wealth and identity is intricate, and navigating it requires self-awareness, introspection, and a commitment to authentic self-discovery.

By recognizing the influence of wealth on your identity, striving for authenticity, and prioritizing values and well-being over materialism, you can develop a healthy and resilient sense of self.

In the chapters ahead, we will continue to explore the psychology of wealth and provide guidance on achieving financial success while nurturing a balanced and authentic identity in an ever-evolving world.

Chapter 43

Coping with Financial Loss

The sensitive and challenging topic of coping with financial loss. Financial setbacks are an inevitable part of life, and how we navigate them can profoundly impact our mental, emotional, and financial well-being. In this chapter, we'll explore the psychology behind coping with financial loss, strategies for resilience, and steps to rebuild your financial stability while maintaining a positive outlook.

Understanding Financial Loss

1. Types of Financial Loss

Financial loss can come in various forms, including job loss, investment declines, business setbacks, or unexpected expenses.

2. Emotional Impact

It often leads to a range of emotions, such as fear, anxiety, sadness, and frustration, which can be challenging to manage.

3. Personal Identity

Financial loss can shake one's sense of self-worth and personal identity, particularly if they closely tied their identity to their financial success.

4. Coping Strategies

Effective coping strategies can help individuals navigate the emotional and practical aspects of financial loss.

The Emotional Impact of Financial Loss

1. Grief and Loss

Financial loss can trigger a grieving process, with stages that may include denial, anger, bargaining, depression, and acceptance.

2. Stress and Anxiety

It often leads to heightened stress and anxiety, affecting overall well-being and decision-making.

3. Self-Esteem

Financial loss can negatively impact self-esteem, as individuals may blame themselves for their financial setbacks.

4. Social Relationships

It can strain social relationships, as financial stress may lead to conflicts and isolation.

Strategies for Coping with Financial Loss

1. Seek Emotional Support

Reach out to friends, family, or support groups to share your feelings and seek emotional support during difficult times.

2. Financial Assessment

Conduct a thorough financial assessment to understand the extent of your loss and create a realistic action plan.

3. Self-Compassion

Practice self-compassion and avoid self-blame, recognizing that financial setbacks are a part of life.

4. Stress Management

Implement stress management techniques such as meditation, exercise, or mindfulness to reduce anxiety and improve resilience.

5. Reevaluate Financial Goals

Reevaluate your financial goals and priorities, adjusting them based on your current circumstances and values.

6. Professional Guidance

Consider seeking guidance from financial advisors or counselors to develop a plan for rebuilding your financial stability.

Rebuilding Financial Stability

1. Budgeting and Saving

Implement a strict budget and savings plan to gradually rebuild your financial resources.

2. Diversify Investments

Diversify your investments to spread risk and reduce vulnerability to future financial losses.

3. Develop New Skills

Explore opportunities to develop new skills or pursue alternative income sources to enhance financial stability.

4. Emergency Fund

Build and maintain an emergency fund to provide a financial safety net for unexpected expenses.

The Rewards of Resilience

1. Emotional Strength

Coping with financial loss builds emotional strength and resilience, preparing you to face future challenges with confidence.

2. Financial Recovery

With time and commitment, many individuals can recover financially and regain their stability.

3. Enhanced Financial Literacy

Navigating financial loss often leads to an enhanced understanding of financial principles and better money management.

4. Personal Growth

Coping with financial loss can foster personal growth and a deeper appreciation for life's non-material aspects.

Conclusion

Coping with financial loss is a challenging journey that requires emotional resilience, self-compassion, and practical strategies.

By seeking support, managing stress, and taking proactive steps to rebuild your financial stability, you can emerge from financial setbacks stronger and more resilient than before. Remember that financial loss does not define your worth, and your journey toward recovery can lead to personal growth and a more balanced perspective on life.

In the chapters ahead, we will continue to explore the psychology of wealth and provide guidance on achieving financial success while nurturing your mental, emotional, and social well-being.

Chapter 44

The Psychology of Homeownership

The fascinating psychology behind homeownership and the profound impact it can have on individuals and families. For many, owning a home is not just a financial transaction but an emotional and psychological journey. In this chapter, we'll delve into the various aspects of the psychology of homeownership, its benefits, challenges, and the emotional significance of having a place to call your own.

The Emotional Significance of Home

1. Sense of Belonging

Homeownership often provides a sense of belonging and roots, as it represents stability and permanence.

2. Personal Expression

Your home can be a canvas for personal expression, reflecting your style, values, and identity.

3. Emotional Security

A home offers emotional security, providing a safe and familiar haven for you and your loved ones.

4. Achievement and Pride

Achieving homeownership can instill a sense of pride and accomplishment, representing a significant life milestone.

The Benefits of Homeownership

1. Financial Investment

Owning a home is often considered a sound financial investment, with potential for long-term appreciation.

2. Stability and Control

Homeownership provides stability and a sense of control over your living environment.

3. Equity and Wealth Building

As you pay down your mortgage, you build equity, contributing to your overall wealth.

4. Emotional Well-being

A well-maintained home can positively impact your emotional well-being, creating a sense of comfort and sanctuary.

The Challenges of Homeownership

1. Financial Responsibility

Owning a home comes with financial responsibilities, including mortgage payments, property taxes, and maintenance costs.

2. Stress and Maintenance

Home maintenance and unexpected repairs can be a source of stress and financial strain.

3. Market Fluctuations

The real estate market can be unpredictable, affecting the value of your home and your financial stability.

4. Emotional Attachment

Overattachment to your home can make it challenging to adapt to changing circumstances, such as downsizing or relocating.

Strategies for Positive Homeownership Experience

1. Financial Preparedness

Before buying a home, ensure you are financially prepared for the responsibilities and potential challenges.

2. Emotional Attachment

Maintain a healthy emotional attachment to your home while recognizing that it is just one aspect of your life.

3. Maintenance Plan

Develop a maintenance plan to address regular upkeep and unforeseen repairs, preventing stress and financial strain.

4. Adaptability

Stay adaptable and open to change, as life circumstances may require adjustments to your homeownership situation.

The Rewards of Homeownership

1. Stability and Security

Homeownership provides stability and security, contributing to your overall well-being and peace of mind.

2. Wealth Building

It offers opportunities for wealth building and financial security over the long term.

3. Personal Expression

Your home can be a canvas for personal expression, allowing you to create a space that reflects your identity and values.

4. Emotional Fulfillment

A well-loved home can bring emotional fulfillment, nurturing a sense of belonging and contentment.

Conclusion

The psychology of homeownership is a rich and complex journey that goes beyond bricks and mortar. It encompasses emotions, dreams, financial decisions, and a sense of belonging.

By understanding the emotional significance, benefits, and challenges of homeownership, you can navigate this path with confidence and enjoy the rewards it brings to your life. Whether you're considering homeownership or have already embarked on this journey, remember that your home is not just a physical space—it's a reflection of your identity, values, and the place where cherished memories are made.

In the chapters ahead, we will continue to explore the psychology of wealth and provide guidance on achieving financial success while nurturing your mental, emotional, and social well-being.

Chapter 45

Wealth and Philanthropy

The meaningful relationship between wealth and philanthropy. Philanthropy, the act of giving to promote the welfare of others, goes hand in hand with financial success for many individuals and families. In this chapter, we'll delve into the psychology behind philanthropy, its impact on both donors and recipients, and strategies for incorporating philanthropy into your wealth journey.

The Psychology of Philanthropy

1. Empathy and Compassion

Philanthropy often arises from empathy and compassion, as individuals seek to alleviate the suffering of others.

2. Gratitude

Gratitude for one's own abundance can inspire acts of philanthropy, as individuals recognize the privilege of their wealth.

3. Legacy and Impact

Many philanthropists are motivated by a desire to leave a lasting legacy and make a positive impact on society.

4. Social Connection

Philanthropy fosters social connections, as donors engage with causes and communities they care about.

The Impact of Philanthropy

1. Positive Change

Philanthropy has the power to create positive change, addressing critical issues such as poverty, education, healthcare, and environmental conservation.

2. Personal Fulfillment

Donors often experience personal fulfillment and a sense of purpose through their philanthropic efforts.

3. Social Influence

Philanthropy can influence social norms and inspire others to engage in charitable activities.

4. Legacy and Recognition

Generous philanthropy can leave a lasting legacy and result in public recognition and honors.

Strategies for Effective Philanthropy

1. Define Your Values

Identify the causes and issues that align with your values and passions, ensuring your philanthropy is personally meaningful.

2. Set Clear Goals

Establish clear philanthropic goals, whether it's a specific amount to give, a cause to support, or an impact you want to achieve.

3. Research and Select Organizations

Conduct thorough research to select reputable organizations and causes that align with your philanthropic goals.

4. Diversify Giving

Consider diversifying your philanthropic efforts across multiple causes and organizations to maximize impact.

5. Time and Expertise

In addition to financial contributions, consider donating your time and expertise to causes in need of your skills.

6. Involve Family and Loved Ones

Involve family members and loved ones in your philanthropic activities, fostering shared values and a sense of community.

The Rewards of Philanthropy

1. Personal Fulfillment

Philanthropy brings personal fulfillment, as donors witness the positive impact of their contributions.

2. Social Connection

It fosters social connection and a sense of belonging within communities that share your philanthropic values.

3. Legacy and Impact

Philanthropy allows you to leave a meaningful legacy and make a lasting impact on the causes you care about.

4. Positive Change

By engaging in philanthropy, you become an agent of positive change, contributing to a better world.

Conclusion

Philanthropy is a powerful force for good that allows individuals to make a positive impact on society while experiencing personal fulfillment and leaving a meaningful legacy.

By understanding the psychology behind philanthropy, setting clear goals, and aligning your giving with your values and passions, you can embark on a rewarding philanthropic journey that not only enriches the lives of others but also adds depth and purpose to your own wealth story.

In the chapters ahead, we will continue to explore the psychology of wealth and provide guidance on achieving financial success while nurturing your mental, emotional, and social well-being through acts of generosity and philanthropy.

Chapter 46

Financial Resilience

The invaluable concept of financial resilience. In a world marked by economic uncertainties and unexpected challenges, financial resilience is the ability to bounce back from setbacks and maintain your financial well-being. In this chapter, we'll delve into the psychology of financial resilience, its significance, strategies for building it, and how it can empower you to navigate life's financial ups and downs with confidence.

Understanding Financial Resilience

1. Adaptability

Financial resilience is about adaptability and the capacity to adjust to changing circumstances without experiencing a significant decline in your financial health.

2. Emotional Strength

It involves emotional strength and the ability to manage stress, anxiety, and uncertainty related to finances.

3. Preparedness

Financial resilience is linked to being prepared for unexpected events and having a plan in place to address financial challenges.

4. Long-Term Sustainability

It goes beyond short-term financial stability and focuses on the long-term sustainability of your financial well-being.

The Importance of Financial Resilience

1. Uncertainty

In an uncertain world, financial resilience provides a sense of security and confidence in facing the unknown.

2. Reducing Stress

It reduces financial stress, allowing you to focus on your overall well-being and goals.

3. Opportunity Seizing

Financial resilience enables you to seize opportunities and take calculated risks to improve your financial situation.

4. Maintaining Independence

It helps maintain financial independence and reduces reliance on external support in times of crisis.

Strategies for Building Financial Resilience

1. Emergency Fund

Establish and maintain an emergency fund to cover unexpected expenses and provide a financial safety net.

2. Debt Management

Address and manage your debt responsibly, avoiding high-interest loans and focusing on a plan for repayment.

3. Diversify Income

Explore multiple income streams to reduce reliance on a single source of income, creating financial stability.

4. Budgeting and Planning

Create a realistic budget and financial plan that aligns with your goals and includes saving for future needs.

5. Financial Education

Invest in your financial education to make informed decisions and adapt to changing financial landscapes.

6. Mindful Spending

Practice mindful spending by distinguishing between needs and wants, avoiding impulsive purchases, and prioritizing long-term financial goals.

7. Insurance

Ensure you have appropriate insurance coverage to protect against unforeseen events such as accidents, illness, or property damage.

The Rewards of Financial Resilience

1. Peace of Mind

Financial resilience provides peace of mind, knowing that you can face financial challenges with confidence and a plan in place.

2. Freedom to Explore

It allows you the freedom to explore opportunities, take risks, and pursue your goals without excessive financial worry.

3. Reduced Stress

Financial resilience reduces overall stress related to money and promotes better mental and emotional well-being.

4. Long-Term Security

By building financial resilience, you ensure long-term financial security and the ability to withstand economic downturns.

Conclusion

Financial resilience is a valuable skill that empowers you to navigate life's financial uncertainties with confidence and grace. By understanding the importance of financial resilience, adopting proactive strategies, and cultivating a mindset that embraces adaptability and preparedness, you can build a strong financial foundation that supports your overall well-being and future aspirations.

In the chapters ahead, we will continue to explore the psychology of wealth and provide guidance on achieving financial success while nurturing your mental, emotional, and social well-being through financial resilience.

Chapter 47

Wealth and Personal Growth

The profound connection between wealth and personal growth. While wealth can certainly provide financial security and comfort, it also serves as a catalyst for personal development and self-discovery. In this chapter, we'll delve into the psychology behind how wealth can fuel personal growth, the challenges it presents, and strategies for leveraging your financial success to become the best version of yourself.

Wealth as a Catalyst for Personal Growth

1. Expanded Opportunities

Wealth can provide access to a wide range of opportunities for learning, growth, and self-improvement.

2. Confidence Building

Financial success can boost your self-confidence and belief in your abilities to overcome challenges.

3. Pursuit of Passions

Wealth enables you to pursue your passions, interests, and hobbies that contribute to personal fulfillment.

4. Lifelong Learning

It encourages lifelong learning and the continuous quest for knowledge and personal development.

The Challenges of Wealth and Personal Growth

1. Complacency

Excessive wealth can lead to complacency, where individuals stop pushing themselves to grow and improve.

2. Materialism

An excessive focus on material possessions can hinder personal growth by prioritizing the acquisition of things over personal development.

3. External Validation

Relying on external markers of success, such as wealth, can overshadow the importance of inner growth and self-acceptance.

4. Identity Confusion

Sudden wealth or significant financial changes can lead to identity confusion as individuals grapple with their new financial reality.

Strategies for Leveraging Wealth for Personal Growth

1. Set Personal Goals

Define personal growth goals that align with your values, passions, and aspirations, alongside your financial objectives.

2. Invest in Learning

Allocate resources to personal development, including education, workshops, and experiences that nurture growth.

3. Embrace Philanthropy

Engage in philanthropy and giving back as a means of personal growth, fostering empathy, and a sense of purpose.

4. Seek Mentorship

Seek mentorship and guidance from individuals who have achieved both financial success and personal growth.

5. Cultivate Self-awareness

Practice self-awareness and self-reflection to understand how wealth impacts your personal growth journey.

6. Balance Material and Personal Goals

Strike a balance between pursuing material wealth and personal development, ensuring both align with your values.

The Rewards of Balancing Wealth and Personal Growth

1. Fulfillment and Contentment

Balancing wealth and personal growth leads to a sense of fulfillment and contentment in your life journey.

2. Resilience

Personal growth fosters emotional and psychological resilience, helping you navigate life's challenges with grace.

3. Authenticity

It promotes authenticity and a deep understanding of your true self, independent of external markers of success.

4. Legacy of Impact

By combining wealth and personal growth, you can leave a legacy of positive impact on the world.

Conclusion

Wealth is not just about financial assets; it's a platform for personal growth, self-discovery, and the pursuit of a more fulfilling and purposeful life.

By recognizing the potential for personal growth within your financial journey, setting meaningful goals, and embracing strategies that align with your values, you can unlock the transformative power of wealth to become the best version of yourself.

In the chapters ahead, we will continue to explore the psychology of wealth and provide guidance on achieving financial success while nurturing your mental, emotional, and social well-being through the lens of personal growth.

Chapter 48

Navigating Economic Downturns

The art of navigating economic downturns with resilience, wisdom, and optimism. In our ever-changing economic landscape, experiencing periods of economic challenges is not uncommon. However, how you respond to these downturns can significantly impact your financial well-being and overall quality of life. In this chapter, we'll delve into the psychology behind navigating economic downturns, share strategies to weather financial storms, and provide guidance on emerging from them even stronger.

Understanding Economic Downturns

1. Inevitability

Economic downturns are a natural part of the economic cycle, characterized by reduced economic activity, job losses, and financial uncertainty.

2. Emotional Impact

They often trigger a range of emotions, including fear, anxiety, and uncertainty, which can affect decision-making and mental well-being.

3. Financial Challenges

Economic downturns can lead to financial challenges such as reduced income, decreased savings, and investment losses.

4. Resilience Opportunity

Navigating economic downturns offers an opportunity to build resilience, adaptability, and financial acumen.

The Psychology of Navigating Economic Downturns

1. Mindset Matters

A positive and proactive mindset is crucial for effectively navigating economic downturns, as it can lead to better decision-making and emotional well-being.

2. Emotional Resilience

Developing emotional resilience is key to managing the stress and anxiety associated with economic uncertainty.

3. Financial Planning

Creating a detailed financial plan helps you assess your current situation, set priorities, and make informed decisions.

4. Adaptability

Flexibility and adaptability are essential skills during economic downturns, as they allow you to pivot and explore new opportunities.

Strategies for Navigating Economic Downturns

1. Emergency Fund

Maintain a well-funded emergency fund to cover essential expenses during periods of reduced income or unexpected expenses.

2. Budgeting

Create a revised budget that reflects your current financial situation and focuses on essential expenses.

3. Debt Management

Prioritize debt management and consider consolidating or negotiating debt terms to alleviate financial pressure.

4. Skill Development

Invest in skill development and professional growth to enhance your employability and income potential.

5. Diversify Income

Explore multiple income streams, including part-time work, freelancing, or entrepreneurship, to increase financial stability.

6. Asset Protection

Protect your assets through diversified investments and appropriate insurance coverage.

7. Emotional Support

Seek emotional support from friends, family, or support groups to cope with stress and anxiety.

The Rewards of Navigating Economic Downturns

1. Resilience

Successfully navigating economic downturns builds resilience, which serves you well in future challenges.

2. Financial Wisdom

You gain valuable financial wisdom and experience that can enhance your financial decision-making.

3. Adaptability

Adaptability becomes a second nature, allowing you to seize opportunities and thrive in various circumstances.

4. Improved Financial Health

By effectively managing economic downturns, you can emerge with improved financial health and stability.

Conclusion

Economic downturns are an inevitable part of our economic reality, but they need not define your financial future. With the right mindset, emotional resilience, and strategic planning, you can navigate these challenging times with grace and emerge even stronger on the other side. Remember that economic downturns can provide valuable lessons, opportunities for growth, and a chance to reassess your financial priorities.

In the chapters ahead, we will continue to explore the psychology of wealth and provide guidance on achieving financial success while nurturing your mental, emotional, and social well-being, even in the face of economic uncertainties.

Chapter 49

Money and the Pursuit of Passion

The delightful intersection of money and the pursuit of your passions. For many, the dream of aligning one's livelihood with their passions is a powerful motivator. In this chapter, we'll delve into the psychology behind how money can support your pursuit of passion, share strategies for turning your passions into a sustainable career, and celebrate the joy that comes from doing what you love.

The Power of Passion-Driven Living

1. Fulfillment

Pursuing your passions can bring a profound sense of fulfillment, as it allows you to engage in activities that resonate deeply with your heart and soul.

2. Motivation

Passion serves as a powerful motivator, driving you to overcome obstacles and persist in the face of challenges.

3. Creativity

Passion ignites creativity, enabling you to approach problems with fresh perspectives and innovative solutions.

4. Authenticity

Living your passions fosters authenticity, as it aligns your actions with your true self and values.

Money as a Catalyst for Passion

1. Financial Freedom

Having a stable financial foundation provides the freedom to explore your passions without the constant worry of making ends meet.

2. Investment in Skills

Money can be invested in acquiring the skills and knowledge necessary to excel in your chosen field of passion.

3. Resource Mobilization

Financial resources can be leveraged to create and market products or services related to your passion.

4. Time Allocation

Financial security allows you to allocate more time to your passions, dedicating hours to practice, creation, or exploration.

Challenges on the Path of Passion

1. Financial Uncertainty

Pursuing passion may involve financial uncertainty, especially during the initial stages of transition.

2. Balancing Act

Balancing financial stability with the pursuit of passion can be challenging, requiring careful planning and decision-making.

3. Patience and Persistence

Building a successful passion-driven career often requires patience and persistent effort.

4. Financial Planning

Effective financial planning is essential to mitigate potential risks and ensure long-term sustainability.

Strategies for Monetizing Your Passion

1. Market Research

Conduct thorough market research to identify opportunities and assess demand for your passion-related products or services.

2. Skill Development

Invest in developing the necessary skills and expertise to excel in your chosen field of passion.

3. Business Planning

Create a solid business plan that outlines your passion-based venture's goals, target audience, and financial projections.

4. Multiple Income Streams

Consider diversifying your income streams, combining your passion with complementary revenue sources.

5. Financial Prudence

Exercise financial prudence by managing expenses, setting aside savings, and creating a safety net for unexpected financial setbacks.

The Rewards of Pursuing Your Passion

1. Deep Fulfillment

Living your passions brings a profound sense of fulfillment and a feeling that your life has purpose and meaning.

2. Resilience

Passion-driven individuals often exhibit resilience, as they are motivated to overcome challenges and continue to grow.

3. Innovation

Passion fosters innovation, allowing you to bring fresh ideas and creativity to your chosen field.

4. Financial Success

With dedication and smart financial planning, pursuing your passion can lead to financial success and stability.

Conclusion

Money can be a powerful ally in the pursuit of your passions, enabling you to lead a life rich in fulfillment and authenticity.

By understanding the symbiotic relationship between money and passion, and by strategically harnessing financial resources to support your dreams, you can embark on a rewarding journey that blends work and passion seamlessly.

In the chapters ahead, we will continue to explore the psychology of wealth and provide guidance on achieving financial success while nurturing your mental, emotional, and social well-being through the pursuit of your deepest passions.

Chapter 50

Wealth and Family Dynamics

The intricate interplay between wealth and family dynamics. Money, as a significant aspect of our lives, has the power to influence family relationships, values, and overall well-being. In this chapter, we'll delve into the psychology behind wealth's impact on family dynamics, share strategies for fostering healthy financial conversations, and celebrate the importance of nurturing strong family bonds amidst the complexities of wealth.

Wealth's Influence on Family Dynamics

1. Values and Priorities

Wealth often shapes family values and priorities, impacting decisions related to education, lifestyle, and philanthropy.

2. Power Dynamics

Money can influence power dynamics within families, potentially leading to tensions or imbalances.

3. Communication Patterns

Wealth can either facilitate open and constructive communication or hinder it, depending on how it's managed and discussed.

4. Generational Impact

Wealth's impact extends across generations, influencing the financial attitudes and behaviors of children and grandchildren.

The Psychology of Family Wealth

1. Expectations

Family members may have varying expectations regarding the use and distribution of wealth, which can lead to conflicts.

2. Identity and Self-Worth

Individuals may tie their identity and self-worth to their family's wealth or their ability to preserve it.

3. Responsibility

Wealth can bring a sense of responsibility to protect, grow, and pass it on to future generations.

4. Legacy

Many families aspire to create a lasting legacy through their wealth, which shapes their financial decisions.

Strategies for Navigating Wealth and Family Dynamics

1. Open and Honest Communication

Foster a culture of open and honest communication within your family, where financial matters can be discussed without judgment or secrecy.

2. Establish Shared Values

Work together as a family to identify and establish shared values and goals related to wealth, philanthropy, and financial priorities.

3. Define Roles and Responsibilities

Clearly define roles and responsibilities within the family concerning wealth management, ensuring transparency and accountability.

4. Educate and Prepare

Invest in financial education for family members to ensure they have the knowledge and skills to manage wealth responsibly.

5. Seek Professional Guidance

Engage financial advisors, estate planners, and therapists when necessary to navigate complex family wealth issues.

6. Encourage Philanthropy

Encourage philanthropic endeavors as a means of bonding and contributing to the greater good together.

The Rewards of Nurturing Family Bonds Amidst Wealth

1. Strong Relationships

Nurturing family bonds amidst wealth fosters strong, supportive relationships built on trust and shared values.

2. Legacy of Unity

A united family can create a lasting legacy that extends beyond wealth, impacting future generations in positive ways.

3. Emotional Wealth

The emotional wealth derived from close family ties often far exceeds the monetary wealth amassed.

4. Collective Purpose

When families align their wealth with a collective purpose, they can create a sense of fulfillment and shared achievement.

Conclusion

Navigating wealth and family dynamics is a delicate yet essential journey.

By understanding the profound influence of wealth on family values, communication patterns, and identity, you can proactively foster a harmonious environment where wealth enriches family bonds rather than strains them.

Remember that the legacy you leave within your family extends beyond financial assets; it encompasses the values, relationships, and shared experiences you create together. In the chapters ahead, we will continue to explore the psychology of wealth and provide guidance on achieving financial success while nurturing your mental, emotional, and social well-being within the context of your family dynamics.

Chapter 51

The Psychology of Luxury

The fascinating world of luxury and the intricate psychology that surrounds it. Luxury, whether in the form of opulent goods, lavish experiences, or exclusive services, has a unique allure that captivates the human psyche. In this chapter, we'll delve into the psychology behind luxury consumption, examine the emotions and motivations that drive it, and explore the implications of incorporating luxury into your life.

The Allure of Luxury

1. Status and Prestige

Luxury often conveys status, prestige, and exclusivity, which can boost one's self-esteem and social standing.

2. Sensory Pleasure

Luxurious experiences and goods often provide heightened sensory pleasure, indulging our senses in ways that are deeply gratifying.

3. Rarity and Scarcity

The rarity and scarcity of luxury items contribute to their desirability, creating a sense of privilege for those who possess them.

4. Symbol of Success

Luxury is frequently seen as a symbol of success, achievement, and personal accomplishment.

The Psychology of Luxury Consumption

1. Emotional Gratification

Consuming luxury can provide a sense of emotional gratification, pleasure, and happiness.

2. Self-Expression

Luxury choices often serve as a means of self-expression, allowing individuals to convey their unique tastes, values, and identities.

3. Social Comparison

Luxury consumption can be driven by the desire to surpass or keep up with others in social and economic circles.

4. Exclusivity and Scarcity

The pursuit of exclusive and scarce luxury items can create a sense of thrill and excitement.

Luxury and Well-Being

1. Hedonic Well-Being

Luxury experiences contribute to hedonic well-being, enhancing the quality of life through pleasure and enjoyment.

2. Eudaimonic Well-Being

Luxury can also contribute to eudaimonic well-being by fostering a sense of purpose, meaning, and self-actualization.

3. Potential Pitfalls

Excessive luxury consumption can lead to hedonic adaptation and financial strain, potentially diminishing overall well-being.

4. Sustainable Luxury

Sustainable luxury options are gaining popularity, as individuals seek to align their consumption with environmental and ethical values.

Strategies for Mindful Luxury Consumption

1. Define Your Values

Identify the values and priorities that matter most to you when it comes to luxury consumption.

2. Budget and Plan

Set a budget for luxury spending and plan your purchases mindfully, considering long-term financial goals.

3. Evaluate Authenticity

Assess the authenticity and meaning behind luxury choices, ensuring they align with your true self.

4. Explore Experiences

Consider prioritizing luxury experiences over material possessions, as they often provide lasting memories and well-being.

5. Practice Gratitude

Cultivate gratitude for the luxuries you enjoy, recognizing and appreciating their positive impact on your life.

The Rewards of Mindful Luxury

1. Enhanced Well-Being

Mindful luxury consumption can contribute to enhanced well-being, both hedonic and eudaimonic.

2. Self-Expression

Luxury choices that align with your values serve as a means of self-expression and authenticity.

3. Financial Freedom

Mindful luxury spending allows you to enjoy the finer things in life without compromising your long-term financial goals.

4. Ethical Consideration

Prioritizing sustainable and ethical luxury options allows you to make choices that benefit both you and the planet.

Conclusion

Luxury, in its various forms, holds a unique place in human experience, offering pleasure, status, and self-expression.

By understanding the psychology of luxury consumption, and by adopting a mindful and values-driven approach, you can enjoy the benefits of luxury while preserving your financial well-being and overall happiness.

Remember that luxury, when chosen consciously and authentically, can be a source of joy and fulfillment, enhancing your well-being and the quality of your life journey.

In the chapters ahead, we will continue to explore the psychology of wealth and provide guidance on achieving financial success while nurturing your mental, emotional, and social well-being, even in the world of luxury.

Chapter 52

Financial Decision Regret

The intriguing topic of financial decision regret. Regret is a common and complex emotion that can arise from choices we make regarding money. In this chapter, we'll explore the psychology behind financial decision regret, examine its causes, consequences, and offer strategies to cope with and learn from these experiences.

Understanding Financial Decision Regret

1. What is Regret?

Regret is a powerful emotion that occurs when we perceive that we made a mistake or made a suboptimal choice in a specific situation.

2. Financial Regret

Financial regret specifically pertains to decisions related to money, such as investments, purchases, or financial planning.

3. Causes of Regret

Financial regret can stem from various factors, including poor outcomes, missed opportunities, or the feeling of not having made the best choice.

4. Universality

Regret is a universal human experience, and almost everyone will encounter it at some point in their financial journey.

The Psychology of Financial Decision Regret

1. Hindsight Bias

Hindsight bias is the tendency to view past decisions as more predictable and obvious than they were at the time.

2. Loss Aversion

Loss aversion makes us more sensitive to losses than gains, amplifying the regret associated with financial losses.

3. Counterfactual Thinking

Counterfactual thinking involves imagining alternative outcomes, often leading to feelings of regret about what might have been.

4. Emotional Impact

Financial decision regret can evoke strong negative emotions, such as disappointment, frustration, or sadness.

Coping with Financial Decision Regret

1. Acknowledge Emotions

Recognize and acknowledge your feelings of regret without judgment. It's a natural response to certain situations.

2. Self-Compassion

Practice self-compassion by treating yourself with kindness and understanding, as you would a friend who made a similar mistake.

3. Reflect and Learn

Reflect on the factors that contributed to the regrettable decision and consider what you can learn from the experience.

4. Avoid Dwelling

While reflection is helpful, avoid dwelling on past regrets, as excessive rumination can be detrimental to your well-being.

5. Seek Professional Advice

If financial decisions have significant consequences, consider seeking advice from financial professionals or advisors.

The Consequences of Handling Regret

1. Emotional Growth

Handling financial decision regret can lead to emotional growth, resilience, and improved decision-making in the future.

2. Better Decision-Making

Reflecting on past regrets can help you make better financial decisions by learning from past mistakes.

3. Improved Well-Being

Effectively coping with regret contributes to better mental and emotional well-being, reducing the burden of negative emotions.

4. Future Success

Using regret as a stepping stone for personal and financial growth can lead to future success and positive outcomes.

Conclusion

Financial decision regret is a natural part of managing money, and it's essential to recognize and address it constructively.

By understanding the psychology behind regret, practicing self-compassion, and using past mistakes as valuable learning experiences, you can navigate your financial journey with greater resilience and wisdom.

Remember that everyone makes financial decisions they wish they could change, but it's how we cope with regret and grow from it that truly matters.

In the chapters ahead, we will continue to explore the psychology of wealth and provide guidance on achieving financial success while nurturing your mental, emotional, and social well-being, even in the face of regret.

Chapter 53

Wealth and Gratitude

The beautiful relationship between wealth and gratitude. Wealth, in its various forms, provides us with many blessings and opportunities. Gratitude, on the other hand, is a profound and transformative emotion that can enhance our well-being and our relationship with wealth. In this chapter, we'll delve into the psychology behind wealth and gratitude, examine the benefits of cultivating a thankful mindset, and explore strategies for infusing gratitude into your financial journey.

The Power of Gratitude

1. What is Gratitude?

Gratitude is the heartfelt acknowledgment of the kindness and blessings we receive, whether from others or from life itself.

2. Cultivating Awareness

Gratitude involves consciously recognizing and appreciating the positive aspects of our lives, no matter how big or small.

3. Impact on Well-Being

Research has shown that practicing gratitude can lead to increased happiness, improved mental health, and enhanced overall well-being.

4. The Gratitude-Wealth Connection

Wealth, when viewed through the lens of gratitude, can bring about a deeper sense of contentment and fulfillment.

The Psychology of Gratitude and Wealth

1. Shifting Perspectives

Gratitude shifts our perspective from what we lack to what we have, fostering contentment and reducing the desire for excessive consumption.

2. Enhanced Resilience

A grateful mindset enhances our emotional resilience, helping us navigate financial challenges with grace and perspective.

3. Improved Relationships

Expressing gratitude can strengthen social bonds, as it deepens connections and fosters trust.

4. Stress Reduction

Practicing gratitude has been linked to reduced stress and anxiety, which can positively impact financial decision making.

Strategies for Cultivating Gratitude with Wealth

1. Daily Gratitude Practice

Start or end your day with a gratitude journal, jotting down things you're thankful for related to your wealth, no matter how small.

2. Mindful Spending

Practice mindful spending by consciously appreciating the value and utility of the items or experiences your wealth affords you.

3. Giving Back

Engage in philanthropic activities and charitable giving to share your wealth with those in need, fostering gratitude and a sense of purpose.

4. Financial Reflection

Regularly reflect on your financial journey, recognizing the milestones and progress you've made.

5. Count Your Non-Material Wealth

Remember that wealth encompasses not only material possessions but also relationships, health, and personal growth.

The Rewards of Infusing Wealth with Gratitude

1. Contentment

Cultivating gratitude with your wealth brings a deep sense of contentment and satisfaction.

2. Emotional Resilience

A gratitude-rich approach to wealth enhances emotional resilience and the ability to weather financial challenges.

3. Stronger Relationships

Gratitude strengthens relationships, as it fosters connection, empathy, and trust.

4. Financial Wisdom

A thankful mindset can lead to wiser financial decisions, informed by a sense of sufficiency and gratitude.

Conclusion

Gratitude has the power to transform your relationship with wealth, enriching your financial journey with contentment, resilience, and a deeper appreciation for life's blessings. By infusing your financial decisions and practices with gratitude, you can create a harmonious and fulfilling wealth experience that goes beyond material possessions.

Remember that wealth, when embraced with gratitude, becomes a source of profound well-being and a tool for making a positive impact on your life and the lives of others.

In the chapters ahead, we will continue to explore the psychology of wealth and provide guidance on achieving financial success while nurturing your mental, emotional, and social well-being through the lens of gratitude.

Chapter 54

Money and the Pursuit of Meaning

The profound relationship between money and the pursuit of meaning in life. While wealth can bring material comfort, many seek a deeper sense of purpose and fulfillment. In this chapter, we'll delve into the psychology behind using money as a means to pursue meaning, examine the benefits of aligning your financial journey with your values, and provide strategies for finding greater significance through your financial choices.

The Quest for Meaning

1. What is Meaning?

Meaning in life is the sense of significance, purpose, and connection to something greater than oneself.

2. Pursuit of Meaning

Many individuals aspire to infuse their lives with meaning, seeking a purposeful existence beyond material wealth.

3. Money and Meaning

Money can be a tool for pursuing meaning by enabling you to make choices aligned with your values and passions.

4. The Psychology of Meaning

A life imbued with meaning is associated with higher life satisfaction, better mental health, and greater overall well-being.

Money as a Tool for Meaning

1. Aligning with Values

Financial resources can be directed toward causes, pursuits, or endeavors that resonate with your values and contribute to a sense of meaning.

2. Freedom and Opportunity

Wealth can provide freedom and opportunity to explore meaningful experiences, such as travel, education, or philanthropy.

3. Contribution to Others

Money can be used to make a positive impact on the lives of others, fostering a sense of meaning through generosity.

4. Pursuit of Passions

Financial security can allow you to pursue your passions and talents, contributing to a more fulfilling life.

Strategies for Pursuing Meaning with Money

1. Define Your Values

Identify your core values and principles to guide your financial decisions toward a more meaningful life.

2. Philanthropy and Giving

Engage in philanthropic activities and charitable giving to support causes you are passionate about.

3. Invest in Personal Growth

Allocate resources for personal development and growth, whether through education, experiences, or mentorship.

4. Reflect on Your Legacy

Consider the legacy you want to leave and how your wealth can contribute to a more meaningful impact on future generations.

5. Seek Purposeful Work

Explore career or entrepreneurial opportunities that align with your passions and values.

The Rewards of Pursuing Meaning with Money

1. Fulfillment

Pursuing meaning through money leads to a deeper sense of fulfillment and purpose in life.

2. Well-Being

A life driven by values and meaning is associated with enhanced mental and emotional well-being.

3. Legacy and Impact

Your financial choices can leave a lasting legacy and positively impact the lives of others.

4. Personal Growth

The pursuit of meaning through wealth often entails personal growth and self-discovery.

Conclusion

Money can be a powerful instrument for realizing a life rich in meaning and purpose. By aligning your financial choices with your values, passions, and desire for significance, you can embark on a transformative journey that transcends material wealth.

Remember that the pursuit of meaning is a deeply personal and evolving process, and your financial resources can play a pivotal role in shaping a life that is both prosperous and purposeful. In the chapters ahead, we will continue to explore the psychology of wealth and provide guidance on achieving financial success while nurturing your mental, emotional, and social well-being through the pursuit of meaning.

Chapter 55

The Role of Faith and Belief in Wealth

The profound impact of faith and belief on one's relationship with wealth. Faith, whether in a higher power, oneself, or the universe, can significantly influence how individuals approach wealth, make financial decisions, and find meaning in their financial journey. In this chapter, we'll delve into the psychology behind faith and belief in the context of wealth, examine the benefits of a faith-driven approach, and explore strategies for incorporating faith into your financial life.

The Power of Faith and belief

1. What is Faith?

Faith is a deeply held belief or trust in something greater than oneself, whether it be a divine force, personal capabilities, or the order of the universe.

2. Role of Belief

Belief in the potential for growth, success, and abundance plays a pivotal role in shaping financial outcomes.

3. Faith and Resilience

Faith often provides individuals with the resilience and determination to overcome financial challenges.

4. Connection to Wealth

One's faith and belief system can profoundly influence their relationship with wealth and money.

Faith's Influence on Wealth

1. Positive Expectations

Faith fosters positive expectations about financial outcomes, influencing behavior and decisions that support those expectations.

2. Goal Achievement

Belief in one's ability to achieve financial goals can be a powerful motivator, driving persistent effort.

3. Coping with Challenges

Faith can help individuals cope with financial setbacks by providing a sense of purpose and perspective.

4. Attracting Opportunities

Some believe that faith can attract opportunities and resources that align with one's beliefs and intentions.

Strategies for Incorporating Faith into Finances

1. Clarify Your beliefs

Reflect on your beliefs about wealth, money, and abundance, and consider how they shape your financial decisions.

2. Align with Values

Ensure that your financial choices align with your core values and beliefs, creating a sense of harmony in your financial life.

3. Set Faith-Driven Goals

Set financial goals that reflect your faith and belief in your ability to achieve them, creating a positive feedback loop.

4. Practice Gratitude

Cultivate gratitude for wealth and abundance in your life, acknowledging the role of faith in its creation.

5. Seek Guidance

Consider seeking guidance from mentors or advisors who share your faith-driven approach to wealth.

The Rewards of Faith-Driven Wealth

1. Confidence

A faith-driven approach to wealth instills confidence in one's financial decisions and abilities.

2. Resilience

Faith equips individuals with the resilience to navigate financial challenges with grace and determination.

3. Purpose and Meaning

Faith can infuse your financial journey with a deeper sense of purpose and meaning.

4. Attracting Abundance

Belief in abundance can attract opportunities and resources that align with your faith-driven intentions.

Conclusion

Faith and belief play a significant role in shaping our relationship with wealth and the outcomes we experience. By embracing a faith-driven approach to finances, you can tap into the power of positive expectations, resilience, and alignment with your values.

Remember that faith is a deeply personal and evolving aspect of your life, and its influence on your financial journey can lead to a richer and more meaningful experience of wealth. In the chapters ahead, we will continue to explore the psychology of wealth and provide guidance on achieving financial success while nurturing your mental, emotional, and social well-being through the lens of faith and belief.

Chapter 56

Wealth and Generational Wealth Transfer

The fascinating dynamics of wealth transfer between generations. Generational wealth involves passing down financial assets, values, and opportunities from one generation to the next. In this chapter, we'll delve into the psychology behind generational wealth transfer, examine its significance, and offer strategies for navigating this process with care, wisdom, and a focus on preserving your family's legacy.

The Significance of Generational Wealth Transfer

1. What is Generational Wealth?

Generational wealth encompasses assets, resources, and values that are passed down from one generation to another.

2. Impact on Family Legacy

Generational wealth transfer can shape a family's legacy and the opportunities available to future generations.

3. Wealth Preservation

Passing down wealth requires careful planning to preserve its value and impact over time.

4. Emotional Connections

Generational wealth often carries emotional significance, reflecting the hard work and values of previous generations.

The Psychology of Generational Wealth Transfer

1. Values and Expectations

Transferring wealth involves aligning family values and managing the expectations of both givers and receivers.

2. Communication

Open and honest communication is crucial for ensuring a smooth wealth transfer process and addressing potential conflicts.

3. Identity and Self-Worth

Both givers and receivers may tie their identity and self-worth to the process and outcomes of generational wealth transfer.

4. Legacy Building

Generational wealth transfer is an opportunity to build and leave a lasting legacy that extends beyond financial assets.

Strategies for Navigating Generational Wealth Transfer

1. Family Conversations

Initiate family conversations about wealth transfer early, focusing on shared values, goals, and expectations.

2. Estate Planning

Work with legal and financial professionals to create a comprehensive estate plan that aligns with your values and goals.

3. Education and Preparation

Ensure that the next generation is educated and prepared to manage inherited wealth responsibly.

4. Philanthropic Endeavors

Consider involving your family in philanthropic endeavors to instill a sense of purpose and responsibility.

5. Regular Review

Periodically review and update your wealth transfer plan to adapt to changing circumstances and family dynamics.

The Rewards of Thoughtful Wealth Transfer

1. Family Unity

Generational wealth transfer can foster unity within families when it aligns with shared values and goals.

2. Legacy Preservation

A well-planned wealth transfer helps preserve and extend your family's legacy for future generations.

3. Financial Security

Inherited wealth can provide financial security and opportunities for personal growth and fulfillment.

4. Social Impact

Generational wealth can be used to make a positive impact on society through philanthropic efforts.

Conclusion

Generational wealth transfer is a significant and complex process that involves more than just financial assets. It carries the weight of family history, values, and the potential to shape the future.

By approaching this process thoughtfully, with open communication and a focus on shared values and goals, you can ensure that your family's legacy continues to thrive for generations to come.

Remember that generational wealth is not just about passing down assets; it's about passing down the values and principles that have guided your family's success and can continue to do so. In the chapters ahead, we will continue to explore the psychology of wealth and provide guidance on achieving financial success while nurturing your mental, emotional, and social well-being through the lens of generational wealth transfer.

Chapter 57
The Impact of Inflation on Wealth Psychology

The intricate relationship between inflation and wealth psychology. Inflation is a fundamental economic concept that can significantly affect your financial well-being and mindset. In this chapter, we'll explore the psychology behind inflation's impact on wealth, examine its effects on financial decision-making and emotions, and provide strategies for navigating inflation's challenges while maintaining a healthy wealth psychology.

Understanding Inflation

1. What is Inflation?

Inflation is the gradual increase in the prices of goods and services over time, leading to a decrease in the purchasing power of money.

2. Impact on Wealth

Inflation erodes the real value of money and assets, affecting the accumulation and preservation of wealth.

3. Rate Variability

Inflation rates can vary over time and across countries, influencing financial planning and decision-making.

4. Psychological Impact

Inflation can evoke various emotional responses and financial behaviors, shaping your wealth psychology.

The Psychology of Inflation's Impact

1. Fear and Anxiety

Inflation can trigger fear and anxiety about the future, particularly regarding retirement and financial security.

2. Adjustment Difficulty

Adjusting to changing prices and inflation can be challenging, affecting budgeting and financial planning.

3. Short-Term vs. Long-Term Thinking

Inflation often prompts a shift between short-term and long-term financial perspectives, impacting investment choices.

4. Psychological Inflation

Psychological inflation refers to the tendency to overestimate the impact of inflation on one's financial situation.

Strategies for Navigating Inflation's Impact

1. Inflation-Adjusted Investments

Consider investments and assets that have the potential to outpace inflation, such as stocks or real estate.

2. Diversification

Diversify your investment portfolio to spread risk and adapt to changing economic conditions.

3. Financial Education

Stay informed about economic trends, inflation rates, and financial strategies to make informed decisions.

4. Long-Term Planning

Embrace a long-term perspective in your financial planning to account for inflation's effects over time.

5. Emergency Fund

Maintain an emergency fund to cushion the impact of unexpected expenses or economic downturns.

The Rewards of Inflation-Aware Wealth Psychology

1. Financial Resilience

An inflation-aware wealth psychology fosters financial resilience, allowing you to weather economic fluctuations.

2. Informed Decision-Making

Being aware of inflation's impact enables informed decision-making that aligns with your financial goals.

3. Reduced Anxiety

Understanding and planning for inflation can reduce anxiety about your financial future.

4. Long-Term Prosperity

By addressing inflation's challenges, you can secure long-term financial prosperity and security.

Conclusion

Inflation is an inherent aspect of the economic landscape that can influence your wealth psychology and financial well-being.

By understanding the psychology behind inflation's impact, staying informed, and implementing sound financial strategies, you can navigate inflation's challenges and build a resilient wealth psychology that leads to long-term financial prosperity.

Remember that inflation is not an insurmountable obstacle; it's a factor to consider in your financial journey, and with the right approach, you can achieve your financial goals and secure your financial future even in the face of rising prices. In the chapters ahead, we will continue to explore the psychology of wealth and provide guidance on achieving financial success while nurturing your mental, emotional, and social well-being in a changing economic landscape.

Chapter 58

Wealth and Social Responsibility

The crucial intersection of wealth and social responsibility. In an interconnected world, individuals and organizations with financial resources have the opportunity to make a positive impact on society. In this chapter, we'll delve into the psychology behind social responsibility in the context of wealth, examine the benefits of aligning your financial journey with societal well-being, and provide strategies for incorporating social responsibility into your wealth management with compassion and purpose.

The Significance of Social Responsibility

1. What is Social Responsibility?

Social responsibility involves making ethical and sustainable choices that contribute to the well-being of society and the environment.

2. Wealth's Impact

Wealth provides the means to influence positive change, address social issues, and support community initiatives.

3. Ethical Considerations

Social responsibility encompasses ethical decision-making, corporate philanthropy, and sustainable business practices.

4. Legacy and Impact

Engaging in social responsibility efforts can shape your legacy and the impact you leave on future generations.

The Psychology of Wealth and Social Responsibility

1. Empathy and Compassion

Socially responsible individuals often exhibit higher levels of empathy and compassion for others in society.

2. Fulfillment and Purpose

Supporting causes aligned with your values and wealth can lead to a deeper sense of fulfillment and purpose.

3. Wealth as a Tool

Wealth is seen as a tool for making a positive impact, leveraging resources to address societal challenges.

4. Community Engagement

Social responsibility often involves active engagement with communities, fostering connections and shared goals.

Strategies for Incorporating Social Responsibility into Wealth Management

1. Define Your Values

Clarify your values and causes that resonate with you, forming the foundation of your social responsibility efforts.

2. Sustainable Investing

Explore sustainable and socially responsible investment options that align with your values and financial goals.

3. Charitable Giving

Commit to charitable giving by allocating a portion of your wealth to support causes and organizations you believe in.

4. Ethical Business Practices

If you're an entrepreneur or business owner, implement ethical and sustainable practices within your organization.

5. Volunteer and Engage

Actively engage in volunteer work and community initiatives to contribute your time and expertise.

The Rewards of Socially Responsible Wealth

1. Sense of Fulfillment

Socially responsible wealth management leads to a deep sense of fulfillment and meaning in your financial journey.

2. Positive Impact

Your financial resources can create a positive impact on society, addressing critical issues and improving lives.

3. Enhanced Legacy

Social responsibility efforts enhance your legacy, leaving a lasting impression of your values and contributions.

4. Stronger Communities

Engaging in social responsibility strengthens communities and fosters a sense of shared responsibility.

Conclusion

Social responsibility is a powerful lens through which to view your wealth, transforming it from a tool for personal gain into a force for positive change.

By aligning your financial decisions with your values, committing to ethical practices, and actively engaging with causes that matter to you, you can infuse your wealth journey with purpose and societal impact. Remember that social responsibility is not an obligation; it's a choice and an opportunity to make a meaningful difference in the world. In the chapters ahead, we will continue to explore the psychology of wealth and provide guidance on achieving financial success while nurturing your mental, emotional, and social well-being through the lens of social responsibility.

Chapter 59

The Psychology of Financial Planning Tools

The fascinating world of financial planning tools and their impact on your wealth psychology. In an era of technological advancement, various digital tools and apps are available to help you manage your finances more effectively. In this chapter, we'll delve into the psychology behind these tools, examine their influence on financial behaviors and mindset, and provide insights into how to maximize their benefits for your financial well-being.

The Significance of Financial Planning Tools

1. What are Financial Planning Tools?

Financial planning tools encompass a wide range of digital applications and software designed to assist individuals in managing their finances.

2. Wealth Management

These tools can aid in budgeting, investing, retirement planning, debt management, and more, contributing to overall wealth management.

3. Accessibility and Convenience

Financial planning tools offer accessibility and convenience, allowing users to monitor their finances anytime, anywhere.

4. Decision Support

They provide valuable insights and data-driven recommendations to inform financial decisions.

The Psychology of Financial Planning Tools

1. Empowerment and Control

Financial tools empower individuals to take control of their financial lives, reducing anxiety and stress related to money management.

2. Goal-Oriented

Using these tools can help individuals set and track financial goals, increasing motivation and commitment.

3. Behavioral Nudges

Many tools incorporate behavioral psychology principles to encourage positive financial habits, such as saving and investing.

4. Data Visualization

Visual representations of financial data can enhance understanding and decision-making, making finances less intimidating.

Strategies for Maximizing Financial Planning Tools

1. Goal Setting

Utilize financial planning tools to set clear and achievable financial goals, both short-term and long-term.

2. Budgeting and Tracking

Regularly monitor your income, expenses, and investments to ensure alignment with your financial objectives.

3. Automation

Take advantage of automation features to streamline savings, investments, and bill payments.

4. Financial Education

Use the educational resources often provided by these tools to enhance your financial literacy.

5. Data Security

Prioritize the security of your financial information by selecting reputable and secure tools.

The Rewards of Effective Tool Utilization

1. Financial Confidence

Using financial planning tools instills confidence in your ability to manage your finances effectively.

2. Improved Decision-Making

Access to real-time data and insights enables better-informed financial decisions.

3. Goal Achievement

Tracking progress toward your financial goals increases the likelihood of achieving them.

4. Reduced Stress

Effective tools can significantly reduce financial stress and anxiety.

Conclusion

Financial planning tools are valuable allies in your journey toward financial success and well-being.

By leveraging these tools wisely, you can gain greater control over your finances, set and achieve meaningful goals, and ultimately enjoy a more secure and satisfying financial life.

Remember that these tools are meant to enhance your financial journey, but the psychology and mindset behind their use play an equally crucial role in your financial well-being. In the chapters ahead, we will continue to explore the psychology of wealth and provide guidance on achieving financial success while nurturing your mental, emotional, and social well-being through effective financial planning and management.

Chapter 60

Wealth and Financial Security

The essential relationship between wealth and financial security. Financial security is a fundamental aspect of well-being, and wealth can play a significant role in achieving and maintaining it. In this chapter, we'll explore the psychology behind financial security, examine how wealth can contribute to it, and provide strategies for enhancing your financial security while nurturing a sense of peace and confidence in your financial journey.

The Significance of Financial Security

1. What is Financial Security?

Financial security refers to the state of having enough resources and stability to meet current and future financial needs and goals.

2. Peace of Mind

It provides peace of mind, reducing anxiety and stress related to financial matters.

3. Wealth's Role

Wealth, whether in the form of savings, investments, or assets, is a critical component of financial security.

4. Emotional Well-Being

Financial security contributes to emotional well-being, allowing individuals to focus on other aspects of their lives.

The Psychology of Financial Security

1. Sense of Control

Financial security fosters a sense of control over one's financial future, reducing feelings of helplessness.

2. Reduced Stress

A secure financial foundation minimizes stress related to unexpected expenses or financial setbacks.

3. Freedom and Choices

It provides the freedom to make choices aligned with one's values and goals, enhancing overall life satisfaction.

4. Confidence

Financial security bolsters confidence in one's ability to weather financial challenges and achieve long-term goals.

Strategies for Enhancing Financial Security

1. Emergency Fund

Maintain an emergency fund to cover unforeseen expenses and unexpected life events.

2. Debt Management

Manage and reduce high-interest debt to free up resources for savings and investments.

3. Savings and Investments

Prioritize regular savings and investments to build a financial safety net for the future.

4. Insurance

Ensure you have appropriate insurance coverage to protect against significant financial losses.

5. Financial Education

Invest in financial education to make informed decisions and enhance your financial literacy.

The Rewards of Financial Security

1. Peace of Mind

Financial security brings peace of mind, allowing you to focus on your goals and aspirations.

2. Resilienc

It equips you with the resilience to face unexpected financial challenges without compromising your well-being.

3. Goal Achievement

With a secure financial foundation, you can confidently work toward and achieve your financial goals.

4. Quality of Life

Financial security enhances your overall quality of life by providing the resources to live comfortably and pursue your passions.

Conclusion

Financial security is a cornerstone of a fulfilling and well-rounded life, and wealth can be a vital tool in building and maintaining it.

By understanding the psychology behind financial security, setting clear goals, and implementing sound financial strategies, you can achieve a greater sense of peace, confidence, and well-being in your financial journey.

Remember that financial security is not solely about accumulating wealth; it's about using your resources wisely to create a stable and fulfilling life for yourself and your loved ones. In the chapters ahead, we will continue to explore the psychology of wealth and provide guidance on achieving financial success while nurturing your mental, emotional, and social well-being through the lens of financial security.

Chapter 61

Money and Mindful Spending

The transformative concept of mindful spending and its profound impact on your relationship with money. In a world where consumerism often encourages impulsive and excessive spending, mindful spending encourages thoughtful, intentional, and values-driven choices. In this chapter, we'll delve into the psychology behind mindful spending, examine its benefits for financial well-being, and provide practical strategies for incorporating mindfulness into your spending habits to achieve greater financial satisfaction and alignment with your life's priorities.

The Significance of Mindful Spending

1. What is Mindful Spending?

Mindful spending involves consciously and intentionally directing your financial resources toward expenses that align with your values and priorities.

2. Consumer Culture

In a consumer-driven culture, mindful spending offers an alternative approach that values experiences and meaning over material possessions.

3. Emotional Fulfillment

Mindful spending seeks to provide emotional fulfillment and satisfaction, reducing the pursuit of happiness through material accumulation.

4. Financial Wellness

It contributes to financial wellness by promoting responsible and conscious financial choices.

The Psychology of Mindful Spending

1. Awareness and Presence

Mindful spending cultivates awareness and presence in your financial decisions, promoting conscious choices.

2. Value Alignment

It encourages you to align your spending with your values, ensuring that your money supports what truly matters to you.

3. Emotional Connection

Mindful spending fosters a deeper emotional connection with your financial resources, enhancing gratitude and contentment.

4. Reduced Impulsivity

By practicing mindfulness, you can reduce impulsive spending and make intentional choices that serve your long-term goals.

Strategies for Incorporating Mindful Spending

1. Reflect on Values

Take time to reflect on your core values and priorities, considering how they relate to your spending habits.

2. Create a Spending Plan

Develop a spending plan or budget that allocates your financial resources in alignment with your values and goals.

3. Delay Gratification

Practice delaying gratification by pausing before making non-essential purchases and considering their alignment with your values.

4. Mindful Purchases

Consciously evaluate each purchase by asking yourself if it truly contributes to your well-being and aligns with your values.

5. Gratitude Practice

Incorporate a gratitude practice into your spending routine, acknowledging the value of the resources you have.

The Rewards of Mindful Spending

1. Financial Alignment

Mindful spending leads to greater financial alignment with your values and priorities.

2. Reduced Financial Stress

By avoiding impulsive and unnecessary purchases, you can reduce financial stress and increase financial well-being.

3. Enhanced Quality of Life

Mindful spending enhances your quality of life by directing resources toward experiences and items that truly matter to you.

4. Sustainable Choices

It promotes sustainability by encouraging responsible consumption and reducing waste.

Conclusion

Mindful spending is a powerful practice that allows you to reclaim control over your financial choices and align your spending with your values and priorities.

By incorporating mindfulness into your spending habits, you can experience greater financial satisfaction, reduce impulsive purchases, and cultivate a deeper sense of gratitude and contentment in your financial journey.

Remember that mindful spending is not about deprivation; it's about making choices that enhance your overall well-being and support a more meaningful and intentional life. In the chapters ahead, we will continue to explore the psychology of wealth and provide guidance on achieving financial success while nurturing your mental, emotional, and social well-being through the lens of mindful spending.

Chapter 62

Wealth and Networking

The significant relationship between wealth and networking. Networking is not just a professional activity; it's a powerful tool that can help you grow your wealth, open up new opportunities, and enhance your financial well-being. In this chapter, we'll delve into the psychology behind networking, examine its impact on wealth accumulation, and provide strategies for building meaningful connections that can enrich your financial journey.

The Significance of Networking

1. What is Networking?

Networking involves building and maintaining relationships with individuals, both personally and professionally, to exchange information, support, and opportunities.

2. Wealth and Opportunities

Networking can create access to new opportunities, potential clients, partners, investors, and valuable insights that can boost your financial prospects.

3. Information Flow

It facilitates the flow of information about market trends, investment opportunities, and business developments.

4. Career Advancemen

Networking can also contribute to career growth and job opportunities, which can ultimately increase your earning potential.

The Psychology of Networking

1. Relationship Building

Networking is fundamentally about building relationships, often based on trust, reciprocity, and shared interests.

2. Social Capital

It enhances your social capital, which can be leveraged to access resources and opportunities that you might not have on your own.

3. Growth Mindset

Networking encourages a growth mindset, fostering a willingness to learn, adapt, and seize opportunities.

4. Emotional Intelligence

Effective networking requires emotional intelligence, including empathy, active listening, and effective communication.

Strategies for Effective Networking

1. Authenticity

Be authentic in your interactions, focusing on building genuine connections rather than transactional relationships.

2. Value Exchange

Offer value to your network by sharing knowledge, resources, and support whenever possible.

3. Diverse Connections

Build a diverse network that includes individuals from various backgrounds, industries, and perspectives.

4. Follow-Up

Nurture your connections through regular follow-up, expressing appreciation and staying engaged.

5. Networking Events

Attend networking events, conferences, and industry gatherings to expand your reach and meet new contacts.

The Rewards of Effective Networking

1. Wealth Growth

Effective networking can lead to wealth growth through new business opportunities, investments, and partnerships.

2. Knowledge Access

It provides access to valuable knowledge and insights that can inform your financial decisions.

3. Career Advancement

Networking can advance your career, leading to promotions and salary increases.

4. Support Network

Your network can serve as a support system during challenging financial times, offering advice, resources, and encouragement.

Conclusion

Networking is not just a professional skill; it's a pathway to wealth growth, career advancement, and personal development.

By understanding the psychology behind networking, practicing authenticity, and nurturing meaningful connections, you can leverage your network to enhance your financial journey and create opportunities that align with your wealth-building goals.

Remember that effective networking is not solely about what you can gain; it's about building mutually beneficial relationships that contribute to your growth and the growth of those around you. In the chapters ahead, we will continue to explore the psychology of wealth and provide guidance on achieving financial success while nurturing your mental, emotional, and social well-being through the lens of networking.

Chapter 63

The Role of Financial Advisors in Wealth Psychology

The pivotal role of financial advisors in shaping and enhancing wealth psychology. Financial advisors are not just experts in managing money; they also play a significant role in guiding their clients toward a healthier and more positive relationship with wealth. In this chapter, we'll delve into the psychology behind the advisor-client relationship, examine the benefits of working with a financial advisor, and provide insights into how this partnership can foster greater financial well-being.

The Significance of Financial Advisors

1. Who Are Financial Advisors?

Financial advisors are professionals who provide guidance and expertise in various aspects of financial planning, investment, and wealth management.

2. Expertise and Experience

They bring specialized knowledge and experience to help clients navigate complex financial decisions.

3. Personalization

Financial advisors tailor their recommendations to clients' unique financial goals, needs, and circumstances.

4. Accountability

They provide accountability and support in staying on track with financial plans and goals.

The Psychology of the Advisor-Client Relationship

1. Trust and Communication

The advisor-client relationship is built on trust, effective communication, and a deep understanding of the client's values and objectives.

2. Emotional Support

Financial advisors offer emotional support during periods of financial stress and uncertainty, helping clients stay focused on long-term goals.

3. Education and Empowerment

They empower clients by educating them about financial concepts, encouraging informed decision-making.

4. Goal Alignment

Financial advisors align clients' financial plans with their life goals, fostering a sense of purpose and direction.

Benefits of Working with a Financial Advisor

1. Holistic Planning

Financial advisors provide comprehensive, holistic financial planning that considers all aspects of a client's financial life.

2. Goal Achievement

They help clients set and achieve financial goals, from buying a home to planning for retirement.

3. Risk Management

Advisors assist in managing financial risks, from market volatility to unexpected life events.

4. Peace of Mind

Working with an advisor can reduce financial anxiety and provide peace of mind that your financial future is in capable hands.

Strategies for a Successful Advisor-Client Relationship

1. Clear Communication

Maintain open and transparent communication with your advisor, sharing your financial concerns and aspirations.

2. Goal Setting

Collaborate with your advisor to set clear and achievable financial goals that align with your values.

3. Regular Reviews

Schedule regular financial check-ins with your advisor to review progress and make necessary adjustments.

4. Trust Your Advisor

Trust the expertise and guidance of your financial advisor, recognizing their role in helping you achieve financial success.

The Rewards of the Advisor-Client Partnership

1. Financial Confidence

Working with a financial advisor can instill confidence in your financial decisions and long-term plans.

2. Financial Success

The guidance of a skilled advisor can lead to greater financial success and security.

3. Emotional Well-Being

A positive advisor-client relationship can contribute to reduced financial stress and enhanced emotional well-being.

4. Time and Freedom

By delegating financial tasks to an advisor, you can enjoy more time and freedom to focus on what matters most to you.

Conclusion

Financial advisors are not just financial experts; they are partners in your journey toward financial well-being.

By understanding the psychology behind the advisor-client relationship, fostering trust, and collaborating effectively, you can harness the expertise of a financial advisor to achieve your financial goals, reduce financial stress, and nurture a healthier wealth psychology.

Remember that seeking guidance from a financial advisor is a proactive step toward securing your financial future and enhancing your overall quality of life. In the chapters ahead, we will continue to explore the psychology of wealth and provide guidance on achieving financial success while nurturing your mental, emotional, and social well-being through the support of trusted financial advisors.

Chapter 64

Wealth and Creativity

The intriguing connection between wealth and creativity. While wealth is often associated with financial prosperity, it can also serve as a catalyst for creativity and innovation. In this chapter, we'll delve into the psychology behind how wealth can influence creativity, examine the reciprocal relationship between the two, and provide insights into how you can harness your wealth to nurture and enhance your creative potential.

The Significance of Creativity

1. What is Creativity?

Creativity is the ability to generate novel ideas, solutions, and expressions that are original and valuable.

2. Wealth as a Facilitator

Wealth can provide resources, time, and freedom to pursue creative endeavors.

3. Creative Expression

Creativity offers an avenue for self-expression and exploration, contributing to personal growth and fulfillment.

4. Innovation and Wealth Creation

Creativity is a driving force behind innovation, which can lead to wealth generation through new products, services, and businesses.

The Psychology of Wealth and Creativity

1. Resource Abundance

Wealth provides access to resources such as education, tools, and experiences that can nurture creativity.

2. Reduced Financial Stress

Financial security, often associated with wealth, can free the mind from the stress of financial instability, allowing creative thinking to flourish.

3. Risk-Taking

Wealth can provide a safety net that encourages risk-taking, a key element in creative exploration.

4. Freedom to Experiment

The financial cushion of wealth can offer the freedom to experiment, explore, and dedicate time to creative pursuits.

Harnessing Wealth for Creativity

1. Pursue Passion Projects

Allocate time and resources to pursue creative passion projects that align with your interests and talents.

2. Invest in Education

Invest in creative education and skill development to enhance your creative abilities.

3. Collaborate and Network

Engage in collaborative efforts and network with creative individuals to gain inspiration and support.

4. Support Creative Causes

Use your wealth to support creative causes, such as arts organizations or educational initiatives, that promote creativity in your community.

The Rewards of Creativity

1. Personal Fulfillment

Creativity fosters personal fulfillment and a sense of purpose, enriching your life beyond financial achievements.

2. Innovation

Creative endeavors can lead to innovations that create value and potentially generate additional wealth.

3. Problem-Solving

Creativity enhances problem-solving skills, aiding in overcoming financial challenges and obstacles.

4. Legacy Building

Creative contributions can leave a lasting legacy, impacting future generations and society as a whole.

Conclusion

Wealth and creativity are intertwined in a dynamic relationship. While wealth can facilitate creativity, creativity, in turn, can lead to innovations that contribute to wealth generation and personal fulfillment.

By recognizing the connection between wealth and creativity and intentionally nurturing your creative potential, you can enrich your financial journey and elevate your overall quality of life.

Remember that creativity is not limited to artistic pursuits; it can manifest in various forms, from entrepreneurship to problem-solving and beyond. In the chapters ahead, we will continue to explore the psychology of wealth and provide guidance on achieving financial success while nurturing your mental, emotional, and social well-being through the lens of creativity.

Chapter 65

The Psychological Impact of Taxation

The complex and often overlooked psychological impact of taxation. While taxes are a fundamental part of our financial lives, their influence extends beyond our bank accounts. In this chapter, we'll explore the psychology behind taxation, examine how it can affect our behavior, emotions, and attitudes, and provide insights into managing the psychological aspects of taxation for a healthier financial outlook.

The Significance of Taxation

1. What is Taxation?

Taxation is the process by which governments collect revenue from individuals and businesses to fund public services and infrastructure.

2. Fiscal Responsibility

Taxes play a crucial role in maintaining public services, social programs, and infrastructure necessary for a well-functioning society.

3. Wealth Redistribution

They can also serve as a means of wealth redistribution, promoting economic fairness and equity.

4. Psychological Influence

Taxes have a significant psychological impact on individuals, influencing their financial decisions and emotional well-being.

The Psychology of Taxation

1. Financial Burden

Taxes can be perceived as a financial burden, affecting disposable income and the ability to meet personal financial goals.

2. Compliance and Trust

The level of trust in the taxation system and perceptions of fairness can influence compliance and tax morale.

3. Behavioral Responses

Taxation can lead to various behavioral responses, such as tax avoidance or evasion, and impact investment decisions.

4. Emotional Impact

Taxes can evoke emotions ranging from frustration and resentment to civic pride and a sense of contribution to society.

Strategies for Managing the Psychological Impact of Taxation

1. Education and Understanding

Enhance your understanding of taxation systems and how they work to make informed financial decisions.

2. Tax Planning

Engage in tax planning to optimize your financial situation while staying compliant with tax laws.

3. Mindful Perspective

Adopt a mindful perspective regarding taxes, focusing on their role in supporting essential public services.

4. Seek Professional Advice

Consult tax professionals or financial advisors to navigate complex tax situations and minimize stress.

The Rewards of Managing Taxation Psychology

1. Financial Peace of Mind

Managing taxation psychology can lead to greater financial peace of mind, reducing stress related to tax-related issues.

2. Compliance and Trust

A positive attitude toward taxation can contribute to higher compliance rates and increased trust in the taxation system.

3. Informed Decision-Making

Understanding taxation allows for more informed financial decisions, optimizing your financial well-being.

4. Civic Engagement

Recognizing the role of taxes in society can foster a sense of civic engagement and contribution to community development.

Conclusion

Taxation is a multifaceted aspect of our financial lives that extends beyond numbers and calculations.

By understanding the psychology behind taxation, educating ourselves on tax systems, and adopting a mindful perspective, we can navigate the financial landscape with greater ease and reduce stress related to tax matters.

Remember that taxation serves as a cornerstone of society, funding essential services and infrastructure that benefit us all. In the chapters ahead, we will continue to explore the psychology of wealth and provide guidance on achieving financial success while nurturing your mental, emotional, and social well-being, including managing the psychological impact of taxation.

Chapter 66

Wealth and Legal Matters

The intricate relationship between wealth and legal matters. While wealth can bring financial security and opportunities, it also carries legal responsibilities and considerations that can significantly impact your financial well-being. In this chapter, we'll delve into the psychology behind legal aspects of wealth, examine their importance, and provide insights into how you can effectively navigate legal matters to protect and enhance your financial journey.

The Significance of Legal Matters

1. Legal Matters and Wealth

Legal matters encompass a wide range of issues, including estate planning, contracts, taxation, and asset protection.

2. Wealth Preservation

Effective legal planning is essential for preserving wealth and ensuring it is passed on to future generations as intended.

3. Risk Mitigation

Legal strategies can mitigate risks, protect assets, and shield your financial interests from potential threats.

4. Peace of Mind

Addressing legal matters can provide peace of mind, knowing that your financial affairs are in order and legally protected.

The Psychology of Legal Matters

1. Emotional Impact

Legal matters can evoke various emotions, from anxiety and uncertainty to relief and empowerment.

2. Decision-Making

The complexity of legal decisions can affect your financial decision-making process and overall well-being.

3. Future Planning

Effective legal planning is closely tied to future planning, including retirement, estate distribution, and legacy building.

4. Family Dynamics

Legal matters can have a significant impact on family dynamics and relationships, necessitating open communication and understanding.

Strategies for Managing Legal Matters

1. Legal Guidance

Seek legal guidance from qualified professionals, such as attorneys and financial advisors, to navigate complex legal issues.

2. Comprehensive Planning

Engage in comprehensive estate planning to ensure your wishes are carried out regarding your assets and legacy.

3. Regular Review

Regularly review and update legal documents, such as wills and trusts, to reflect changes in your financial situation and goals.

4. Open Communication

Foster open communication with family members and beneficiaries to prevent potential conflicts related to legal matters.

The Rewards of Managing Legal Matters

1. Financial Security

Effective legal planning enhances financial security by protecting assets and ensuring their distribution according to your wishes.

2. Peace of Mind

Addressing legal matters provides peace of mind, reducing stress related to uncertainties and potential legal disputes.

3. Family Harmony

Open communication and comprehensive legal planning can foster family harmony and reduce the risk of conflicts.

4. Legacy Preservation

Legal matters play a pivotal role in preserving and passing on your legacy to future generations.

Conclusion

Legal matters are an integral part of managing and protecting your wealth. By understanding the psychology behind legal aspects of wealth, seeking qualified legal guidance, and engaging in comprehensive planning, you can navigate these matters with confidence and ensure that your financial journey is not only prosperous but also secure.

Remember that addressing legal matters is a proactive step toward safeguarding your assets, protecting your legacy, and nurturing a harmonious financial and familial future.

In the chapters ahead, we will continue to explore the psychology of wealth and provide guidance on achieving financial success while nurturing your mental, emotional, and social well-being, including effectively managing legal matters.

Chapter 67

Money and Emotional Resilience

The profound connection between money and emotional resilience. While wealth can provide a sense of financial security, it's not immune to the challenges life throws our way. In this chapter, we'll delve into the psychology behind the relationship between money and emotional resilience, examine the impact of financial stress on well-being, and provide strategies for nurturing emotional resilience in the face of financial ups and downs.

The Significance of Emotional Resilience

1. What is Emotional Resilience?

Emotional resilience is the ability to bounce back from adversity, maintain mental well-being, and adapt to life's challenges.

2. Financial Stress

Financial stress is a common source of adversity that can test emotional resilience.

3. Holistic Well-Being

Emotional resilience is a vital component of holistic well-being, encompassing mental, emotional, and social aspects of life.

4. Coping with Uncertainty

Building emotional resilience equips you with the tools to cope with financial uncertainty and setbacks.

The Psychology of Money and Emotional Resilience

1. Financial Stress and Well-Being

Financial stress can have a significant impact on emotional well-being, leading to anxiety, depression, and other mental health challenges.

2. Financial Stability and Confidence

A sense of financial stability can boost confidence and contribute to emotional resilience.

3. Adaptability and Problem-Solving

Emotionally resilient individuals tend to be more adaptable and effective problem solvers when faced with financial challenges.

4. Coping Strategies

Healthy coping strategies, such as seeking support and maintaining a positive outlook, are essential for emotional resilience.

Strategies for Nurturing Emotional Resilience

1. Financial Planning

Engage in comprehensive financial planning to reduce the risk of unexpected financial crises and enhance peace of mind.

2. Mindfulness Practices

Incorporate mindfulness practices into your daily routine to manage stress and build emotional resilience.

3. Seek Support

Reach out to friends, family, or mental health professionals when facing financial stress to receive emotional support and guidance.

4. Self-Compassion

Practice self-compassion and avoid self-blame during financial difficulties; remember that setbacks are a natural part of life.

The Rewards of Emotional Resilience

1. Mental Well-Being

Emotional resilience contributes to mental well-being, reducing the impact of financial stress on mental health.

2. Positive Outloo

It fosters a positive outlook and a belief in your ability to overcome financial challenges.

3. Stronger Relationships

Emotionally resilient individuals tend to have stronger social connections and healthier relationships.

4. Adaptation and Growth

Emotional resilience enables adaptation and growth, even in the face of financial adversity.

Conclusion

Money and emotional resilience are interconnected aspects of our lives. By understanding the psychology behind this relationship, engaging in proactive financial planning, and adopting healthy coping strategies, you can navigate financial challenges with greater emotional resilience.

Remember that building emotional resilience is an ongoing process that requires self-compassion, support, and a positive outlook.

In the chapters ahead, we will continue to explore the psychology of wealth and provide guidance on achieving financial success while nurturing your mental, emotional, and social well-being, including the development of emotional resilience in your financial journey.

Chapter 68

Wealth and Financial Freedom

The inseparable connection between wealth and financial freedom. Financial freedom is not just a destination; it's a state of mind and a way of life that wealth can help you achieve. In this chapter, we'll delve into the psychology behind financial freedom, explore its significance, and provide insights into how you can use wealth as a tool to attain and savor the true essence of financial freedom.

The Essence of Financial Freedom

1. Defining Financial Freedom

Financial freedom is the ability to make choices and live life on your terms without being constrained by financial concerns.

2. Wealth as a Means

Wealth serves as a means to attain financial freedom, offering you the resources and options to live the life you desire.

3. Quality of Life

Financial freedom enhances your quality of life, allowing you to pursue your passions, spend time with loved ones, and experience personal fulfillment.

4. Peace of Mind

It brings peace of mind by reducing financial stress and anxiety about the future.

The Psychology of Wealth and Financial Freedom

1. Wealth as Security

Accumulating wealth can provide a sense of security and confidence in facing life's uncertainties.

2. Autonomy and Control

Financial freedom empowers you with autonomy and control over your financial decisions and lifestyle.

3. Purpose and Fulfillment

It enables you to align your financial resources with your values and life goals, fostering a sense of purpose and fulfillment.

4. Stress Reduction

Financial freedom can significantly reduce the stress associated with financial constraints.

Strategies for Attaining Financial Freedom

1. Clear Financial Goals

Set clear and achievable financial goals that align with your values and desired lifestyle.

2. Smart Financial Planning

Engage in smart financial planning, including budgeting, saving, and investing, to build wealth steadily.

3. Manage Debt

Effectively manage and reduce debt to free up financial resources for wealth accumulation.

4. Diversify Income Streams

Explore opportunities to diversify your income streams, such as investing in assets or pursuing side ventures.

The Rewards of Financial Freedom

1. Lifestyle Flexibility

Financial freedom provides the flexibility to choose the lifestyle you desire, whether it involves travel, early retirement, or pursuing your passions.

2. Reduced Stress

It significantly reduces financial stress, allowing you to focus on what truly matters in life.

3. Generosity

Financial freedom enables you to be more generous, both with your loved ones and with causes that matter to you.

4. Legacy Building

It offers the opportunity to leave a lasting legacy by supporting future generations and philanthropic endeavors.

Conclusion

Financial freedom is a journey that wealth can help you embark upon, but it's also a state of mind that transcends material possessions. By understanding the psychology behind financial freedom, setting clear goals, and engaging in prudent financial planning, you can work towards a life where financial constraints no longer dictate your choices.

Remember that financial freedom is a deeply personal concept, and it's unique to each individual.

In the chapters ahead, we will continue to explore the psychology of wealth and provide guidance on achieving financial success while nurturing your mental, emotional, and social well-being, including the pursuit and appreciation of financial freedom in your life.

Chapter 69

The Psychology of Charitable Giving

The fascinating world of charitable giving and the profound psychology behind it. Charitable giving is not only an act of generosity but also a reflection of one's values and a source of personal fulfillment. In this chapter, we'll delve into the psychology of charitable giving, examine its significance, and provide insights into how you can incorporate charitable giving into your wealth journey to create a positive impact on both your life and the lives of others.

The Significance of Charitable Giving

1. What is Charitable Giving?

Charitable giving involves donating time, money, or resources to support charitable organizations, causes, or individuals in need.

2. Altruism and Empathy

It reflects a sense of altruism and empathy for the well-being of others.

3. Personal Values

Charitable giving allows individuals to align their financial resources with their personal values and beliefs.

4. Social Impact

It creates a positive impact on society, addressing various social, environmental, and humanitarian issues.

The Psychology of Charitable Giving

1. Emotional Reward

Charitable giving is associated with the release of "feel-good" hormones, such as oxytocin and dopamine, leading to a sense of fulfillment and happiness.

2. Personal Connection

Supporting causes that resonate with your experiences or values can establish a personal connection and a deeper sense of purpose.

3. Social Influence

Social factors, such as peer influence and societal norms, can play a role in charitable giving decisions.

4. Legacy and Impact

Charitable giving provides the opportunity to leave a lasting legacy and make a meaningful impact on the world.

Strategies for Effective Charitable Giving

1. Define Your Values

Identify the causes and issues that align with your values and inspire your charitable giving.

2. Set a Budget

Allocate a portion of your wealth to charitable giving within your overall financial plan.

3. Research and Select Organizations

Thoroughly research charitable organizations to ensure they align with your values and are efficient in their operations.

4. Get Involved

Consider donating not only money but also your time, skills, or expertise to actively contribute to causes you support.

The Rewards of Charitable Giving

1. Personal Fulfillment

Charitable giving fosters personal fulfillment and a sense of purpose, contributing to overall well-being.

2. Social Connection

It can lead to increased social connection and a sense of belonging within a community of like-minded individuals.

3. Positive Impact

Charitable giving creates a positive impact on society, addressing critical issues and making the world a better place.

4. Legacy and Inspiration

It inspires future generations to continue the tradition of giving, leaving a lasting legacy of generosity.

Conclusion

Charitable giving is a powerful way to make a positive impact on both your life and the lives of others.

By understanding the psychology behind charitable giving, defining your values, and actively engaging in thoughtful giving, you can experience a deeper sense of fulfillment and purpose in your wealth journey. Remember that charitable giving is not limited to financial donations; it encompasses various forms of support, including time and expertise.

In the chapters ahead, we will continue to explore the psychology of wealth and provide guidance on achieving financial success while nurturing your mental, emotional, and social well-being, including the art and science of charitable giving in your life.

Chapter 70

Wealth and Personal Branding

The dynamic relationship between wealth and personal branding. Personal branding isn't just for celebrities or influencers; it's a powerful tool that can help you leverage your wealth, expertise, and unique qualities to achieve your goals and make a positive impact on the world. In this chapter, we'll delve into the psychology behind personal branding, discuss its significance, and provide insights into how you can harness it to enhance your wealth journey and leave a lasting impression.

The Essence of Personal Branding

1. What is Personal Branding?

Personal branding is the process of creating and managing a distinctive identity or image that represents you, your values, and your expertise.

2. Wealth as a Catalyst

Wealth can serve as a catalyst for personal branding, providing the resources and opportunities to build a strong and influential brand.

3. Trust and Credibility

A well-crafted personal brand can foster trust and credibility, enabling you to stand out in your field.

4. Impact and Legacy

Personal branding allows you to make a lasting impact on your industry and leave a legacy that extends beyond financial success.

The Psychology of Personal Branding

1. Self-Perception

Personal branding starts with understanding your unique qualities, values, and expertise and how you want to be perceived by others.

2. Building Trust

A consistent and authentic personal brand builds trust with your audience, whether they are clients, colleagues, or the public.

3. Emotional Connection

Effective personal branding creates an emotional connection with your audience, making your message more memorable and impactful.

4. Adaptability and Growth

A strong personal brand can adapt and evolve with your changing goals and circumstances.

Strategies for Effective Personal Branding

1. Self-Reflection

Engage in self-reflection to identify your strengths, values, and unique qualities that will shape your personal brand.

2. Consistency

Maintain consistency in your messaging, image, and actions to build a strong and reliable brand identity.

3. Content Creation

Share your knowledge and expertise through various content platforms, such as blogs, social media, or public speaking.

4. Networking

Build a network of like-minded individuals and professionals who can help amplify your brand and support your goals.

The Rewards of Personal Branding

1. Influence and Impact

An effective personal brand can increase your influence and impact, both in your industry and in society.

2. Career Advancement

It can open doors to career opportunities, collaborations, and leadership roles.

3. Legacy Building

Personal branding allows you to leave a legacy by sharing your knowledge and expertise with others.

4. Personal Fulfillment

The process of personal branding can lead to personal growth and fulfillment as you align your identity with your values and goals.

Conclusion

Personal branding is a powerful tool that can help you leverage your wealth and expertise to achieve your goals, make a positive impact, and leave a lasting legacy.

By understanding the psychology behind personal branding, engaging in self-reflection, and consistently building and nurturing your brand, you can unlock new opportunities and enhance your wealth journey.

Remember that personal branding is not about self-promotion but about authentically sharing your unique qualities and knowledge with the world. In the chapters ahead, we will continue to explore the psychology of wealth and provide guidance on achieving financial success while nurturing your mental, emotional, and social well-being, including the art of personal branding in your life.

Chapter 71

The Emotional toll of Bankruptcy

Where we'll discuss a topic that many find challenging to navigate—the emotional toll of bankruptcy. While bankruptcy is a legal process designed to provide financial relief, it often comes with a heavy emotional burden. In this chapter, we'll delve into the psychological aspects of bankruptcy, explore its significance, and provide insights into how to cope with the emotional challenges that may arise during this difficult time.

Understanding Bankruptcy

1. What is Bankruptcy?

Bankruptcy is a legal proceeding that allows individuals and businesses overwhelmed by debt to seek relief from their financial obligations.

2. Financial Crisis

It is often the result of a significant financial crisis, such as overwhelming medical bills, job loss, or unmanageable credit card debt.

3. Legal Process

Bankruptcy is a legal process that provides individuals with a fresh financial start by discharging certain debts or reorganizing payment plans.

4. Emotional Strain

Bankruptcy can be emotionally challenging, as it involves facing financial difficulties head-on and may come with societal stigma.

The Psychology of Bankruptcy

1. Shame and Stigma

Individuals facing bankruptcy may experience shame and stigma, often driven by societal misconceptions about financial failure.

2. Grief and Loss

The process can trigger emotions akin to grief and loss, as individuals may mourn the financial stability and security they once had.

3. Stress and Anxiety

Bankruptcy can lead to stress and anxiety, stemming from uncertainty about the future and the potential consequences of the process.

4. Relief and Fresh Start

On the positive side, bankruptcy can also provide a sense of relief and a fresh start, offering the opportunity to rebuild one's financial life.

Coping with the emotional Toll

1. Seek Emotional Support

Reach out to friends, family, or a mental health professional to share your feelings and receive emotional support during this challenging time.

2. Financial Education

Educate yourself about the bankruptcy process, understanding your rights and responsibilities, to reduce anxiety and uncertainty.

3. Self-Compassion

Practice self-compassion and avoid self-blame, recognizing that financial difficulties can happen to anyone.

4. Rebuilding and Resilience

Focus on rebuilding your financial life and developing resilience to face future challenges.

The Rewards of Coping with Bankruptcy

1. Emotional Healing

Coping with the emotional toll of bankruptcy can lead to emotional healing and a sense of closure.

2. Financial Recovery

It offers the potential for financial recovery and a more stable financial future.

3. Learning and Growth

Bankruptcy can be a valuable learning experience, providing insights into financial management and resilience.

4. Rebuilding Credit

With time and responsible financial practices, it's possible to rebuild credit and regain financial stability.

Conclusion

Bankruptcy is undeniably a challenging experience, and the emotional toll it takes is significant. However, it's essential to remember that bankruptcy is a legal process designed to offer a fresh start for individuals facing overwhelming debt.

By seeking emotional support, educating yourself about the process, and practicing self-compassion, you can navigate the emotional challenges and move toward a more stable and secure financial future. Remember that bankruptcy does not define your worth or your potential for financial success.

In the chapters ahead, we will continue to explore the psychology of wealth and provide guidance on achieving financial success while nurturing your mental, emotional, and social well-being, including coping with and recovering from the emotional toll of bankruptcy.

Chapter 72

Money and the Quest for Fulfillment

Where we embark on a profound journey, the exploration of money and its intricate relationship with the quest for fulfillment. Money, while a practical tool for financial security and comfort, is often intertwined with our aspirations for a fulfilling and meaningful life. In this chapter, we'll delve into the psychology behind the pursuit of fulfillment, discuss the significance of this quest, and provide insights into how you can balance your financial journey with the pursuit of a more meaningful and fulfilling existence.

The Pursuit of Fulfillment

1. Defining Fulfillment

Fulfillment is the sense of contentment, purpose, and satisfaction that comes from living a meaningful and purpose-driven life.

2. The Role of Money

Money plays a dual role—it provides the means to meet our basic needs and offers opportunities to enhance our sense of fulfillment.

3. Balance and Integration

Achieving a balance between financial stability and personal fulfillment is key to a well-rounded and satisfying life.

4. Psychological Well-being

The quest for fulfillment is closely tied to psychological well-being, encompassing emotional, mental, and social aspects of life.

The Psychology of Money and Fulfillment

1. Financial Security and Peace of Mind

Financial stability can contribute to a sense of peace of mind, reducing stress and anxiety, thus creating fertile ground for fulfillment.

2. Pursuit of Passions and Hobbies

Money can enable us to pursue our passions, hobbies, and interests, enhancing our overall sense of fulfillment.

3. Impact and Contribution

Financial resources can be channeled into causes and initiatives that align with our values, allowing us to make a positive impact on the world.

4. Wealth and Well-being

The relationship between wealth and well-being is complex, and achieving fulfillment goes beyond accumulating wealth.

Strategies for Balancing Money and Fulfillment

1. Reflect on Values and Goals

Take time to reflect on your values, goals, and what truly brings you fulfillment to align your financial journey accordingly.

2. Define Financial Priorities

Establish clear financial priorities that include both short-term necessities and long-term aspirations.

3. Financial Planning

Engage in comprehensive financial planning to ensure that your financial resources support your pursuit of fulfillment.

4. Embrace Mindfulness

Incorporate mindfulness practices into your daily life to remain present, appreciate life's experiences, and enhance your sense of fulfillment.

The Rewards of Balancing Money and Fulfillment

1. Holistic Well-being

Balancing money and fulfillment can lead to holistic well-being, encompassing emotional, mental, and social dimensions of life.

2. Purpose and Meaning

It fosters a sense of purpose and meaning, providing motivation and direction in your life.

3. Personal Growth

Balancing these aspects encourages personal growth and self-awareness, allowing you to continually evolve.

4. Positive Impact

It empowers you to make a positive impact on your life and the lives of others, contributing to a better world.

Conclusion

The quest for fulfillment is a deeply personal and lifelong journey that money can both support and complicate. By understanding the psychology behind money and fulfillment, reflecting on your values and goals, and engaging in mindful financial planning, you can strike a harmonious balance that leads to a more satisfying and meaningful life.

Remember that the pursuit of fulfillment is unique to each individual, and there is no one-size-fits-all approach. In the chapters ahead, we will continue to explore the psychology of wealth and provide guidance on achieving financial success while nurturing your mental, emotional, and social well-being, including the ongoing quest for fulfillment in your life.

Chapter 73

Wealth and Economic Disparities

Where we delve into the complex and critical topic of wealth and economic disparities. Economic disparities, often driven by factors like income inequality, access to opportunities, and systemic biases, have far-reaching effects on societies and individuals. In this chapter, we'll explore the psychology behind economic disparities, discuss their significance, and provide insights into how we can address and mitigate these disparities in a compassionate and equitable manner.

Understanding Economic Disparities

1. What Are Economic Disparities?

Economic disparities refer to the unequal distribution of financial resources, opportunities, and outcomes within a society or community.

2. Causes and Drivers

These disparities can stem from various factors, including income inequality, educational disparities, systemic biases, and historical injustices.

3. Societal Implications

Economic disparities can lead to social inequality, limited access to essential services, and reduced opportunities for marginalized communities.

4. Emotional Impact

The psychological toll of economic disparities includes stress, anxiety, and feelings of injustice, both for those experiencing disparities and those advocating for change.

The Psychology of Economic Disparities

1. Wealth and Well-being

Economic disparities can significantly impact well-being, with individuals experiencing disparities often facing higher stress levels and decreased mental health.

2. Social Comparison

Comparing one's financial situation to others can lead to feelings of inadequacy or superiority, depending on where one falls on the economic spectrum.

3. Empathy and Compassion

Empathy and compassion play a crucial role in addressing disparities by fostering understanding and driving social change.

4. Privilege and Responsibility

Recognizing one's privilege and societal responsibility is essential in promoting equity and reducing disparities.

Strategies for Addressing Economic Disparities

1. Education and Awareness

Promote education and awareness about economic disparities to foster empathy and understanding among individuals and communities.

2. Advocacy and Activism

Engage in advocacy and activism to address systemic issues that perpetuate economic disparities, such as advocating for policy changes and social justice.

3. Financial Literacy

Empower individuals with financial literacy skills to help them navigate economic challenges and make informed decisions.

4. Support Marginalized Communities

Support organizations and initiatives that work to uplift marginalized communities, providing access to resources and opportunities.

The Rewards of Addressing Economic Disparities

1. Social Equity

Efforts to reduce economic disparities contribute to a more equitable society, where everyone has access to opportunities and resources.

2. Enhanced Well-being

Addressing disparities can improve the well-being and mental health of individuals and communities affected by economic inequality.

3. Strengthened Communities

Stronger communities are built through solidarity and a shared commitment to social justice and equity.

4. A More Just Society

Collective action against economic disparities leads to a fairer and more just society for all.

Conclusion

Economic disparities are a pressing issue that impacts individuals and societies on multiple levels. By understanding the psychology behind these disparities, promoting education and awareness, advocating for change, and supporting marginalized communities, we can work towards a more equitable and just world.

Remember that addressing economic disparities is an ongoing journey that requires collective effort and a commitment to empathy, compassion, and social justice.

In the chapters ahead, we will continue to explore the psychology of wealth and provide guidance on achieving financial success while nurturing your mental, emotional, and social well-being, including contributing to the reduction of economic disparities in your life and society.

Chapter 74

The Psychology of Wealth Transfer Planning

Where we embark on a journey into the complex world of wealth transfer planning. Transferring wealth from one generation to the next is a significant financial milestone, but it also carries profound emotional and psychological implications. In this chapter, we'll explore the psychology behind wealth transfer planning, discuss its importance, and provide insights into how to navigate this process while nurturing family relationships and individual well-being.

Understanding Wealth Transfer

1. What is Wealth Transfer?

Wealth transfer is the process of passing assets, financial resources, and sometimes family legacies from one generation to the next.

2. Multifaceted Planning

Wealth transfer planning involves not only financial considerations but also emotional and interpersonal dynamics within families.

3. Goals and Intentions

It centers around defining your goals and intentions for the transfer, whether it's preserving wealth, supporting loved ones, or giving back to the community.

4. Emotional Complexity

Wealth transfer often brings forth complex emotions, such as fear, guilt, and a desire to ensure the financial well-being of heirs.

The Psychology of Wealth Transfer Planning

1. Emotional Barriers

Common emotional barriers to effective wealth transfer planning include fear of conflict, concerns about spoiling heirs, and feelings of guilt or obligation.

2. Family Dynamics

Understanding family dynamics is essential, as differing values and expectations among heirs can lead to tension and misunderstandings.

3. Legacy and Impact

Many individuals desire their wealth to leave a lasting legacy or make a positive impact on future generations or charitable causes.

4. Open Communication

Open and honest communication among family members is a cornerstone of successful wealth transfer planning.

Strategies for Effective Wealth Transfer Planning

1. Start Early

Begin the planning process early to ensure that your intentions are clear, and you have ample time to address any emotional or logistical challenges.

2. Define Values and Goals

Clarify your values, goals, and intentions for the transfer to guide decision-making and align your wealth with your legacy.

3. Involve Heirs

Involve heirs in the planning process, providing an opportunity for them to learn about financial responsibilities and understand your intentions.

4. Seek Professional Guidance

Consult with financial advisors and estate planning professionals to ensure that your wealth transfer plan aligns with your goals and adheres to legal requirements.

The Rewards of Effective Wealth Transfer Planning

1. Family Unity

Successful wealth transfer planning can strengthen family bonds and foster unity by promoting open communication and understanding.

2. Legacy Preservation

It allows for the preservation of family legacies, values, and the impact of your wealth on future generations.

3. Financial Security

Heirs benefit from financial security and a clear understanding of their roles and responsibilities in managing family wealth.

4. Philanthropic Contributions

Wealth transfer planning can facilitate philanthropic contributions, allowing families to give back to causes that matter to them.

Conclusion

Wealth transfer planning is not just a financial transaction; it's a deeply personal and emotional journey that carries significant meaning for both you and your heirs.

By understanding the psychology behind wealth transfer, defining your values and goals, involving heirs in the process, and seeking professional guidance, you can navigate this complex terrain while nurturing family relationships and individual well-being.

Remember that effective wealth transfer planning is an ongoing process that evolves with your family's needs and aspirations. In the chapters ahead, we will continue to explore the psychology of wealth and provide guidance on achieving financial success while nurturing your mental, emotional, and social well-being, including the art of wealth transfer planning in your life.

Chapter 75

Money and Personal Boundaries

Where we delve into the intricate relationship between money and personal boundaries. Personal boundaries are the emotional and psychological limits we establish to protect our well-being and maintain healthy relationships. Money, with its multifaceted roles in our lives, often intersects with these boundaries. In this chapter, we'll explore the psychology behind money and personal boundaries, discuss their significance, and provide insights into how you can strike a balance that promotes financial well-being and healthy relationships.

Understanding Personal Boundaries

1. What Are Personal Boundaries?

Personal boundaries are the limits we set on how we allow others to treat us, what we accept, and how we protect our emotional and mental well-being.

2. Types of Boundaries

Boundaries can encompass physical, emotional, and financial aspects of our lives, including how we handle money and interact with others regarding financial matters.

3. Significance of Boundaries

Healthy personal boundaries are essential for maintaining self-respect, protecting our emotional health, and fostering balanced relationships.

4. Role of Money

Money often becomes intertwined with personal boundaries when it involves lending, borrowing, sharing expenses, or navigating financial disagreements with loved ones.

The Psychology of Money and Personal Boundaries

1. Financial Independence

Establishing financial boundaries can promote independence and self-reliance, allowing individuals to make decisions that align with their values and goals.

2. Empowerment

Personal boundaries empower individuals to assert themselves in financial matters, ensuring that their financial interests are protected.

3. Conflict Resolution

Clear boundaries can prevent financial conflicts and provide a framework for resolving financial disagreements within relationships.

4. Respect and Communication

Mutual respect and open communication are crucial when discussing and negotiating financial boundaries with loved ones.

Strategies for Setting and Maintaining Financial Boundaries

1. Self-Reflection

Take time to self-reflect and identify your financial values, priorities, and boundaries.

2. Open Communication

Engage in open and honest communication with loved ones about your financial boundaries, expectations, and shared financial responsibilities.

3. Assertiveness

Practice assertiveness in financial matters, expressing your needs and boundaries while respecting the needs and boundaries of others.

4. Seek Professional Help

If necessary, seek guidance from financial advisors or therapists who can help you navigate complex financial boundary issues.

The Rewards of Healthy Financial Boundaries

1. Emotional Well-being

Healthy financial boundaries contribute to emotional well-being, reducing stress and conflict related to money.

2. Stronger Relationships

Clear financial boundaries can strengthen relationships by promoting mutual understanding and respect.

3. Financial Stability

Establishing financial boundaries helps individuals maintain financial stability and make informed financial decisions.

4. Personal Growth

Setting and maintaining healthy financial boundaries can lead to personal growth, increased self-awareness, and improved financial literacy.

Conclusion

Balancing money and personal boundaries is essential for financial well-being and maintaining healthy relationships. By understanding the psychology behind these boundaries, engaging in open communication, and practicing assertiveness, you can navigate the intersection of money and personal boundaries with confidence and grace. Remember that personal boundaries are not rigid but can evolve and adapt as circumstances change. In the chapters ahead, we will continue to explore the psychology of wealth and provide guidance on achieving financial success while nurturing your mental, emotional, and social well-being, including the art of setting and maintaining healthy financial boundaries in your life.

Chapter 76

Wealth and the Art of Negotiation

Where we delve into the fascinating world of wealth and the art of negotiation. Negotiation is a skill that transcends financial transactions; it's a powerful tool for achieving financial success, resolving conflicts, and building mutually beneficial relationships. In this chapter, we'll explore the psychology behind negotiation, discuss its significance in wealth management, and provide insights into how you can master the art of negotiation to enhance your financial well-being.

The Essence of Negotiation

1. What is Negotiation?

Negotiation is a dynamic and interactive process where two or more parties engage in discussions to reach mutually acceptable agreements.

2. Everyday Application

Negotiation is a part of our daily lives, from salary discussions and business deals to resolving disputes with family and friends.

3. Wealth Implications

Effective negotiation can directly impact your wealth by influencing your income, investments, expenses, and financial decisions.

4. Psychology of Negotiation

Understanding the psychological aspects of negotiation, such as persuasion and empathy, can significantly enhance your negotiation skills.

The Psychology of Negotiation

1. Interpersonal Dynamics

Negotiation involves complex interpersonal dynamics, including power dynamics, emotions, and the need to build trust.

2. Persuasion and Influence

The art of negotiation includes the ability to persuade and influence others while also being open to influence yourself.

3. Creativity and Problem-Solving

Successful negotiators often employ creative problem-solving techniques to find win-win solutions.

4. Conflict Resolution

Negotiation is a powerful tool for resolving conflicts, whether they are financial disputes or interpersonal disagreements.

Strategies for Mastering Negotiation

1. Preparation

Thoroughly prepare for negotiations by researching, setting clear objectives, and anticipating potential objections.

2. Active Listening

Practice active listening to understand the needs and perspectives of the other party, fostering empathy and rapport.

3. Win-Win Approach

Strive for win-win solutions that benefit all parties involved, as these tend to lead to more sustainable agreements.

4. Emotional Intelligence

Develop emotional intelligence to navigate the emotional aspects of negotiation effectively.

The Rewards of Mastering Negotiation

1. Financial Gain

Effective negotiation can lead to increased income, better investment deals, and reduced expenses, all contributing to financial success.

2. Conflict Resolution

It equips you with the skills to resolve conflicts, preventing them from escalating and potentially harming your financial well-being.

3. Building Relationships

Successful negotiation can foster positive relationships and collaborations that open doors to future opportunities.

4. Empowerment

Mastering negotiation empowers you to advocate for your financial interests and make informed decisions.

Conclusion

The art of negotiation is a valuable skill that can empower you to achieve your financial goals, resolve conflicts, and build meaningful relationships. By understanding the psychology behind negotiation, preparing effectively, practicing active listening, and striving for win-win solutions, you can become a skilled negotiator who can navigate the complexities of wealth management with confidence.

Remember that negotiation is a skill that can be honed over time, and every negotiation provides an opportunity for growth and learning. In the chapters ahead, we will continue to explore the psychology of wealth and provide guidance on achieving financial success while nurturing your mental, emotional, and social well-being, including the mastery of negotiation in your financial journey.

Chapter 77
The Psychological Impact of Financial Windfalls

Where we explore the intriguing psychological impact of financial windfalls. A financial windfall, whether it's an unexpected inheritance, a lottery win, or a significant bonus, can be a life-altering event that brings both opportunities and challenges. In this chapter, we'll delve into the psychology behind windfalls, discuss their emotional and cognitive effects, and provide insights into how to navigate and maximize the benefits of sudden financial abundance.

Understanding Financial Windfalls

1. What Are Financial Windfalls?

Financial windfalls are unexpected and substantial sums of money that significantly exceed your usual income or assets.

2. Common Windfall Sources

Windfalls can come from various sources, including inheritances, lotteries, investments, and unexpected career opportunities.

3. Mixed Emotions

While windfalls often evoke excitement and joy, they can also trigger anxiety, guilt, and complex emotional responses.

4. Psychological Impact

The psychological impact of a financial windfall extends beyond immediate financial considerations and can influence your overall well-being.

The Psychology of Financial Windfalls

1. Emotional Rollercoaster

Windfalls can create an emotional rollercoaster, ranging from euphoria and relief to anxiety and fear of mismanagement.

2. Cognitive Challenges

Managing a windfall can be cognitively challenging, as it requires making complex financial decisions and addressing personal goals.

3. Impact on Relationships

Windfalls can strain or strengthen relationships, depending on how they are managed and communicated within the family or social circle.

4. Identity and Self-Worth

The sudden influx of wealth can prompt questions about identity and self-worth, as individuals grapple with their newfound financial status.

Strategies for Navigating Financial Windfalls

1. Pause and Reflect

Take time to pause and reflect on your values, goals, and the impact of the windfall on your life.

2. Seek Professional Advice

Consult with financial advisors and professionals to create a comprehensive financial plan that aligns with your objectives.

3. Consider Tax Implications

Be mindful of tax implications, as windfalls may have tax consequences that need to be addressed.

4. Address Emotional Needs

Address the emotional aspects of receiving a windfall by seeking support from therapists or counselors, especially if you experience emotional turbulence.

The Rewards and Challenges of Financial Windfalls

1. Financial Opportunities

Windfalls offer unique financial opportunities, such as debt reduction, investments, or pursuing lifelong dreams.

2. Emotional Growth

Navigating a windfall can lead to emotional growth and self-awareness, as individuals grapple with newfound wealth's impact on their lives.

3. Enhanced Lifestyle

A well-managed windfall can lead to an enhanced lifestyle and increased financial security for you and your loved ones.

4. Responsible Stewardship

The challenge lies in responsible stewardship—ensuring that the windfall benefits you and future generations while preserving your financial well-being.

Conclusion

Receiving a financial windfall is a momentous event that can bring profound changes to your life. By understanding the psychology behind windfalls, seeking professional guidance, addressing emotional needs, and making thoughtful financial decisions, you can navigate the complexities of sudden wealth with grace and wisdom.

Remember that a financial windfall is not just about wealth but also about the opportunities it presents for personal growth, philanthropy, and enhancing your overall well-being. In the chapters ahead, we will continue to explore the psychology of wealth and provide guidance on achieving financial success while nurturing your mental, emotional, and social well-being, including the management of financial windfalls in your financial journey.

Chapter 78

Wealth and Retirement Happiness

Where we explore the delightful intersection of wealth and retirement happiness. Retirement is a significant life transition that offers the promise of newfound freedom and leisure. How you navigate your finances during retirement can significantly impact your overall happiness and well-being. In this chapter, we'll delve into the connection between wealth and retirement happiness, discuss key factors that influence this relationship, and provide insights into how you can maximize your retirement enjoyment while ensuring financial security.

The Dynamics of Retirement Happiness

1. The Quest for Happiness

Retirement is often seen as an opportunity to prioritize happiness and well-being over career and financial obligations.

2. Financial Security

Adequate financial security in retirement is a cornerstone of happiness, as it provides peace of mind and the freedom to pursue your passions.

3. Psychological Adjustment

Retirement can be a period of psychological adjustment, as individuals adapt to new routines, social circles, and financial dynamics.

4. Purpose and Fulfillment

Retirement offers a chance to rediscover or redefine your sense of purpose and find fulfillment in different aspects of life.

Wealth and Its Role in Retirement Happiness

1. Financial Freedom

Wealth accumulated throughout your working years provides the financial freedom to enjoy retirement to the fullest.

2. Lifestyle Choices

Financial resources allow retirees to make lifestyle choices that align with their preferences, from travel and hobbies to volunteering and philanthropy.

3. Health and Well-being

Financial security can positively impact physical and mental health during retirement, reducing stress and enhancing overall well-being.

4. Legacy and Generosity

Wealth can also enable retirees to leave a legacy or engage in acts of generosity that bring a deep sense of satisfaction.

Strategies for Retirement Happiness

1. Financial Planning

Engage in comprehensive financial planning to ensure your retirement nest egg supports your desired lifestyle and goals.

2. Pursue Passions

Explore your passions, interests, and hobbies during retirement, as they can provide a sense of purpose and fulfillment.

3. Stay Connected

Maintain and cultivate social connections to combat feelings of isolation and promote happiness in retirement.

4. Giving Back

Consider opportunities for giving back through volunteering or philanthropy, which can be personally fulfilling.

The Rewards of Retirement Happiness

1. Fulfillment

Retirement happiness can lead to a profound sense of fulfillment and contentment during this life stage.

2. Health Benefits

Happiness in retirement can contribute to improved physical and mental health, enhancing overall well-being.

3. Positive Relationships

Retirement happiness often fosters positive relationships with family, friends, and communities.

4. Legacy and Impact

A happy retirement can leave a lasting legacy and inspire others to prioritize their own well-being.

Conclusion

Retirement is an opportunity to savor the fruits of your labor, pursue your passions, and find happiness in everyday life. By understanding the connection between wealth and retirement happiness, engaging in financial planning, and prioritizing your well-being, you can embark on a fulfilling retirement journey that offers both financial security and emotional richness.

Remember that retirement is a unique and deeply personal chapter in your life story, and with thoughtful planning and a focus on happiness, it can be one of the most rewarding phases of your journey. In the chapters ahead, we will continue to explore the psychology of wealth and provide guidance on achieving financial success while nurturing your mental, emotional, and social well-being, including the pursuit of retirement happiness in your financial journey.

Chapter 79

Money and Financial Independence

We embark on a journey into the empowering world of money and financial independence. Financial independence is a goal that many aspire to, as it offers the freedom to make choices that align with your values and aspirations. In this chapter, we'll explore the significance of financial independence, discuss the steps to achieve it, and provide insights into how you can cultivate a sense of financial freedom that empowers you to live life on your terms.

The Meaning of Financial Independence

1. Defining Financial Independence

Financial independence is the state where your passive income and assets cover your living expenses, freeing you from reliance on a traditional job.

2. Freedom of Choice

It grants you the freedom to make choices based on your desires rather than financial necessity, whether it's pursuing a passion, traveling, or spending time with loved ones.

3. Psychological Impact

Financial independence can have a profound psychological impact, reducing stress, increasing happiness, and enhancing your overall well-being.

4. Personalized Goals

Achieving financial independence allows you to set and prioritize personalized life goals, aligning your financial resources with your aspirations.

The Path to Financial Independence

1. Financial Planning

Comprehensive financial planning is essential to assess your current financial situation, set goals, and create a roadmap to achieve independence.

2. Budgeting and Saving

Budgeting and disciplined saving are key components of building the financial foundation necessary for independence.

3. Investment and Passive Income

Investing wisely to generate passive income streams, such as dividends or rental income, is crucial for achieving financial independence.

4. Debt Management

Managing and reducing debt is essential, as it can erode your ability to accumulate wealth and achieve financial freedom.

Strategies for Cultivating Financial Independence

1. Set Clear Goals

Define your financial independence goals and create a plan to work towards them, breaking them down into achievable milestones.

2. Live Below Your Means

Practice living below your means to increase savings and investments, accelerating your journey to financial independence.

3. Diversify Income Streams

Diversify your sources of income to reduce reliance on a single job or investment, increasing financial stability.

4. Continual Learning

Invest in financial education to make informed decisions and adapt to changing economic conditions.

The Rewards of Financial Independence

1. Freedom and Flexibility

Financial independence offers the freedom to choose how you spend your time and the flexibility to pursue your passions.

2. Reduced Stress

It can significantly reduce financial stress, contributing to better mental and emotional well-being.

3. Legacy and Generosity

Financial independence provides the means to leave a legacy, support loved ones, and engage in philanthropy.

4. Personal Growth

Achieving financial independence often leads to personal growth, increased self-confidence, and a sense of accomplishment.

Conclusion

Financial independence is a goal worth pursuing, as it empowers you to live life on your terms, make choices that align with your values, and prioritize your well-being. By understanding the meaning of financial independence, setting clear goals, and implementing sound financial strategies, you can embark on a fulfilling journey toward financial freedom.

Remember that the path to financial independence is unique to each individual and can evolve over time as your goals and circumstances change. In the chapters ahead, we will continue to explore the psychology of wealth and provide guidance on achieving financial success while nurturing your mental, emotional, and social well-being, including the pursuit of financial independence in your financial journey.

Chapter 80

The Role of Social Support in Wealth Psychology

Where we dive into the vital role of social support in wealth psychology. Money and wealth are not solitary pursuits; they are deeply intertwined with our social connections and relationships. In this chapter, we'll explore the significance of social support in wealth management, discuss how it impacts our financial well-being, and provide insights into how you can leverage the power of your social network to achieve financial success while nurturing your mental, emotional, and social health.

The Importance of Social Support

1. Building Wealth is Not Isolated

Achieving financial success often requires collaboration, advice, and emotional support from friends, family, mentors, and professional networks.

2. Emotional Well-being

Social support provides a crucial emotional safety net during financial challenges, reducing stress and anxiety.

3. Accountability and Motivation

Your social network can help keep you accountable to your financial goals and provide motivation to stay on track.

4. Knowledge and Resources

Access to the knowledge and resources of your social circle can be instrumental in making informed financial decisions.

The Impact of Social Support on Wealth Psychology

1. Peer Influence

Your social circle can influence your financial attitudes, behaviors, and goals, either positively or negatively.

2. Emotional Resilience

Strong social support enhances emotional resilience, helping you navigate financial setbacks and challenges.

3. Networking Opportunities

Social connections often lead to networking opportunities, career growth, and financial collaborations.

4. Shared Financial Goals

Aligning financial goals with your social network can create a sense of shared purpose and cooperation.

Strategies for Leveraging Social Support

1. Open Communication

Maintain open and honest communication with your loved ones about financial matters, encouraging understanding and support.

2. Seek Financial Mentors

Seek mentors or financial advisors within your network who can provide guidance and expertise.

3. Share Knowledge

Share your financial knowledge and resources with others to create a culture of learning and empowerment.

4. Collaborate on Financial Goals**

Collaborate with friends or family members on joint financial goals or investments, fostering teamwork and accountability.

The Rewards of Social Support in Wealth Psychology

1. Emotional Well-being

Strong social support contributes to emotional well-being, reducing stress and enhancing overall life satisfaction.

2. Financial Success

Social support can accelerate your path to financial success by providing valuable insights, resources, and opportunities.

3. Positive Relationships

Nurturing positive social connections can lead to richer, more meaningful relationships with those who share your financial journey.

4. Generosity and Philanthropy

A supportive network often encourages acts of generosity and philanthropy, amplifying the impact of your wealth.

Conclusion

Social support is a powerful force in wealth psychology, playing a significant role in your financial well-being and overall happiness. By recognizing the importance of social connections, fostering open communication, seeking mentors, and collaborating with your network on financial goals, you can harness the collective strength of your social support system to achieve financial success while nurturing your mental, emotional, and social health.

Remember that wealth is not just about accumulating assets but also about the meaningful connections and relationships that enrich your life along the way. In the chapters ahead, we will continue to explore the psychology of wealth and provide guidance on achieving financial success while nurturing your holistic well-being, including the crucial role of social support in your financial journey.

Chapter 81

Wealth and Risk Management

Where we delve into the essential topic of wealth and risk management. Building and preserving wealth is a journey filled with opportunities and challenges, and effective risk management is a critical component of ensuring your financial well-being. In this chapter, we will explore the significance of risk management in wealth accumulation, discuss various types of financial risks, and provide insights into strategies that can help you navigate these risks while protecting your wealth.

The Significance of Risk Management

1. Wealth Preservation

Risk management is vital for safeguarding the wealth you have worked hard to accumulate, preventing unexpected losses.

2. Goal Achievement

Effective risk management ensures that your financial goals and aspirations remain achievable, even in the face of uncertainties.

3. Peace of Mind

Having a robust risk management strategy provides peace of mind, reducing stress and anxiety related to financial matters.

4. Adaptability

Risk management allows you to adapt to changing economic conditions and unexpected life events.

Types of Financial Risks

1. Market Risk

Market fluctuations, such as Stock market volatility, can impact the value of your investments.

2. Credit Risk

Lending or investment defaults can lead to the loss of principal or interest income.

3. Inflation Risk

The erosion of purchasing power due to inflation can reduce the real value of your wealth over time.

4. Longevity Risk

Outliving your retirement savings can be a significant risk, particularly with increasing life expectancies.

Strategies for Effective Risk Management

1. Diversification

Diversifying your investments across different asset classes can help spread risk and reduce vulnerability to market fluctuations.

2. Asset Allocation

Strategically allocating assets based on your risk tolerance and financial goals can mitigate market volatility.

3. Insurance

Utilizing various forms of insurance, such as life, health, and disability insurance, can protect against unexpected events.

4. Emergency Fund

Maintaining an emergency fund provides a financial cushion to handle unforeseen expenses or income interruptions.

The Rewards of Effective Risk Management

1. Wealth Preservation

Effective risk management safeguards your wealth, preventing substantial losses during economic downturns.

2. Financial Security

It enhances your financial security and resilience, allowing you to maintain your lifestyle even when faced with challenges.

3. Confidence in Goals

Having a well-thought-out risk management plan instills confidence that your financial goals can be achieved.

4. Legacy and Generosity

Risk management ensures that you have the means to leave a legacy for future generations or engage in acts of generosity.

Conclusion

Risk is an inherent aspect of wealth accumulation, but with careful planning and effective risk management, you can navigate these challenges while preserving and growing your wealth. By recognizing the significance of risk management, diversifying your investments, utilizing insurance as a protective measure, and maintaining financial reserves, you can create a robust strategy that empowers you to achieve your financial goals with confidence and peace of mind.

Remember that risk management is an ongoing process, and periodically reviewing and adjusting your strategies is essential as your financial circumstances and goals evolve. In the chapters ahead, we will continue to explore the psychology of wealth and provide guidance on achieving financial success while nurturing your holistic well-being, including the art of effective risk management in your financial journey.

Chapter 82

The Psychology of Financial Mistakes

Where we explore the fascinating realm of the psychology of financial mistakes. In our financial journeys, we are bound to encounter moments where we make decisions that don't align with our best interests. Understanding the psychology behind these financial missteps can be a valuable tool for personal growth and improved financial decision-making. In this chapter, we'll delve into the intricacies of financial mistakes, their underlying psychological factors, and how you can learn from them to make wiser financial choices.

The Nature of Financial Mistakes

1. Common Occurrences

Financial mistakes are a natural part of life, and everyone, regardless of financial acumen, makes them from time to time.

2. Impact on Well-being

These mistakes can have varying degrees of impact on your financial well-being, depending on their magnitude and timing.

3. Learning Opportunities

Each financial mistake provides an opportunity for learning, self-reflection, and personal growth.

4. Psychological Factors

Psychological factors often play a significant role in the decisions that lead to financial missteps.

The Psychology Behind Financial Mistakes

1. Cognitive Biases

Cognitive biases, such as confirmation bias and overconfidence, can lead to flawed decision-making by favoring information that confirms preexisting beliefs.

2. Emotional Influences

Emotions, such as fear, greed, and impulsivity, can cloud judgment and lead to impulsive financial choices.

3. Mental Accounting

Mental accounting involves compartmentalizing money into different categories, which can lead to suboptimal decisions.

4. Present Bias

Present bias refers to the tendency to prioritize immediate gratification over long-term benefits, often leading to spending beyond means.

Strategies for Learning and Growth

1. Self-awareness

Develop self-awareness by recognizing your personal financial triggers and biases that may lead to mistakes.

2. Financial Education

Invest in financial education to improve your understanding of money management and investment strategies.

3. Seeking Advice

Seek advice from financial experts or mentors when facing major financial decisions or uncertainties.

4. Mindfulness

Practice mindfulness to enhance your ability to make deliberate, conscious financial choices.

The Rewards of Learning from Financial Mistakes

1. Improved Decision-making

Learning from financial mistakes equips you with the knowledge and wisdom to make better financial decisions in the future.

2. Emotional Resilience

It enhances emotional resilience by reducing the stress and anxiety associated with financial errors.

3. Financial Growth

Over time, applying lessons from past mistakes can contribute to financial growth and stability.

4. Personal Growth

Each mistake becomes an opportunity for personal growth, self-discovery, and increased financial confidence.

Conclusion

Financial mistakes are a natural part of the human experience, but they need not define your financial journey. By understanding the psychology behind these mistakes, developing self-awareness, seeking financial education, and practicing mindfulness, you can transform these errors into valuable stepping stones toward financial wisdom and success.

Remember that the path to financial well-being is not linear, and the lessons learned from your financial mistakes are an integral part of your journey toward financial mastery. In the chapters ahead, we will continue to explore the psychology of wealth and provide guidance on achieving financial success while nurturing your mental, emotional, and social well-being, including the invaluable lessons gained from financial missteps in your financial journey.

Chapter 83

Money and Resilience in Adversity

Where we embark on a profound exploration of the relationship between money and resilience in the face of adversity. Life is filled with unexpected challenges, and your financial well-being can significantly impact your ability to weather these storms and emerge stronger. In this chapter, we will delve into the critical role that money plays in building resilience, discuss strategies to enhance your financial fortitude, and explore how adversity can be a catalyst for personal and financial growth.

The Intersection of Money and Resilience

1. Financial Security

Financial security provides a safety net during adversity, reducing stress and anxiety associated with economic uncertainties.

2. Adaptive Capacity

Financial resources empower you to adapt to changing circumstances, whether it's a job loss, medical emergency, or other unexpected events.

3. Emotional Well-being

Adequate financial resilience can enhance emotional well-being, promoting mental health during challenging times.

4. Long-term Perspective

Financial resilience encourages a long-term perspective, enabling you to focus on your future despite short-term setbacks.

Building Financial Resilience

1. Emergency Fund

Maintaining an emergency fund is a cornerstone of financial resilience, offering a financial cushion to handle unexpected expenses.

2. Debt Management

Managing and reducing debt can increase your financial flexibility and reduce stress during adversity.

3. Diversified Income

Having multiple income streams, such as investments or side hustles, enhances your financial resilience.

4. Financial Planning

Engaging in comprehensive financial planning ensures that your financial goals remain achievable, even in adverse conditions.

Adversity as a Catalyst for Growth

1. Learning and Adaptation

Adversity often leads to valuable lessons, fostering adaptability and continuous learning in your financial journey.

2. Strength and Resilience

Overcoming financial challenges can boost your inner strength and resilience, preparing you for future hardships.

3. Reevaluation of Priorities

Adversity can prompt a reevaluation of your financial priorities, helping you align your resources with what truly matters.

4. Empathy and Generosity

Going through tough times can increase empathy and generosity, as you may become more inclined to help others in need.

The Rewards of Financial Resilience

1. Peace of Mind

Financial resilience offers peace of mind, reducing the stress associated with financial uncertainty.

2. Confidence

It enhances financial confidence, allowing you to face adversity with a sense of control and optimism.

3. Long-term Prosperity

By weathering adversity, you can position yourself for long-term financial prosperity and success.

4. Personal Growth

Financial resilience often leads to personal growth, increased self-confidence, and a deeper understanding of your financial capabilities.

Conclusion

Adversity is an inevitable part of life, but with strong financial resilience, you can not only survive but thrive during challenging times. By recognizing the importance of financial security, building resilience through strategies such as emergency funds and debt management, and embracing adversity as a catalyst for growth, you can fortify your financial well-being and emerge from challenges stronger than before.

Remember that resilience is a trait that can be cultivated and strengthened over time, and your journey toward financial and personal growth is a testament to your inner strength and determination. In the chapters ahead, we will continue to explore the psychology of wealth and provide guidance on achieving financial success while nurturing your mental, emotional, and social well-being, including the indispensable role of financial resilience in your financial journey.

Chapter 84

Wealth and Long-Term Planning

Where we embark on a journey into the realm of wealth and long-term planning. Building and preserving wealth is not just about immediate gains; it's also about securing your financial future and leaving a lasting legacy. In this chapter, we will explore the significance of long-term planning, discuss its impact on wealth accumulation, and provide insights into strategies that can help you chart a path toward enduring financial prosperity.

The Importance of Long-Term Planning

1. Future Security

Long-term planning is essential for ensuring your financial security and peace of mind in the years to come.

2. Legacy Buildin

It allows you to create a legacy for your loved ones or support causes that are dear to your heart.

3. Goal Achievement

Long-term planning helps you turn your financial goals and aspirations into a reality, step by step.

4. Adaptability

A well-thought-out long-term plan equips you to adapt to changing circumstances and economic conditions.

Elements of Effective Long-Term Planning

1. Clear Financial Goals

Define clear and specific financial goals, both short-term and long-term, to guide your planning efforts.

2. Asset Allocation

Strategically allocate your assets based on your risk tolerance and time horizon, aligning your investments with your long-term objectives.

3. Retirement Plannin

Plan for retirement by determining how much you need to save, selecting appropriate retirement accounts, and establishing a timeline.

4. Estate Plannin

Consider estate planning to ensure that your wealth is transferred according to your wishes and with minimal tax implications.

Strategies for Successful Long-Term Planning

1. Regular Review

Regularly review and adjust your long-term plan as your life circumstances, goals, and the financial landscape evolve.

2. Professional Guidanc

Seek advice from financial advisors or planners to create a comprehensive long-term strategy tailored to your unique situation.

3. Patience and Discipline

Practice patience and discipline in adhering to your long-term plan, even in the face of short-term market fluctuations.

4. Contingency Planning

Include contingency plans in your long-term strategy to address unexpected events and ensure you stay on course.

The Rewards of Long-Term Planning

1. Financial Security

Long-term planning provides financial security, enabling you to enjoy a comfortable retirement and pursue your life's passions.

2. Legacy and Generosity

It empowers you to leave a meaningful legacy and engage in acts of generosity, supporting future generations and causes you care about.

3. Peace of Mind

Having a well-defined long-term plan offers peace of mind, knowing that your financial future is secure.

4. Goal Achievement

Long-term planning ensures that your financial goals and dreams can be realized over time, providing a sense of accomplishment.

Conclusion

Long-term planning is a cornerstone of financial success and security. By recognizing the importance of planning for the future, setting clear financial goals, and implementing strategies that align with your aspirations, you can pave the way for enduring wealth and a fulfilling financial journey. Remember that long-term planning is not a static process; it requires periodic evaluation and adjustments as life unfolds.

Your commitment to long-term planning reflects your dedication to securing your financial future and making a lasting impact on the world around you. In the chapters ahead, we will continue to explore the psychology of wealth and provide guidance on achieving financial success while nurturing your mental, emotional, and social well-being, including the integral role of long-term planning in your financial journey.

Chapter 85

The Emotional Side of Investing

Where we embark on an exploration of the emotional facets of investing. Investing is not just about financial strategies and market analysis; it's also deeply intertwined with our emotions, beliefs, and behaviors. In this chapter, we will delve into the significance of emotions in investing, examine common emotional biases that affect investment decisions, and provide insights into how you can navigate the emotional roller coaster of the financial markets while making informed investment choices.

Emotions and Their Impact on Investing

1. Fear and Anxiety

Fear of loss and anxiety about market fluctuations can lead to impulsive selling and missed opportunities.

2. Greed and Overconfidence

Greed and overconfidence can result in chasing high-risk investments and overlooking potential downsides.

3. Regret Aversion

Avoiding the regret of making a wrong decision can lead to a reluctance to sell underperforming investments.

4. Herd Mentality

Following the crowd can cause investors to make decisions based on others' actions rather than their own research.

Common Emotional Biases in Investing

1. Confirmation Bias

Investors tend to seek information that confirms their preexisting beliefs, potentially leading to biased decisions.

2. Loss Aversion

The fear of losses often leads investors to hold onto losing investments longer than they should.

3. Anchoring

Anchoring occurs when investors fixate on a reference point, such as a purchase price, and are reluctant to adjust their outlook accordingly.

4. Overreaction and Underreaction

Emotions can cause investors to overreact to short-term market events or underreact to significant long-term trends.

Strategies for Navigating Emotions in Investing

1. Self-awareness

Recognize your emotional triggers and biases to make more rational investment decisions.

2. Diversification

Diversify your investment portfolio to reduce the impact of emotional reactions to individual assets.

3. Long-term Perspective

Maintain a long-term perspective and resist the temptation to make impulsive changes based on short-term market fluctuations.

4. Investment Education

Invest in your investment education to make informed decisions and better understand the rationale behind your investments.

The Rewards of Emotionally Intelligent Investing

1. Better Decision-making

Emotionally intelligent investing leads to better decision-making, potentially resulting in improved investment outcomes.

2. Reduced Stress

By managing emotions effectively, you can reduce the stress and anxiety associated with investment decisions.

3. Long-term Success

Emotionally intelligent investors often achieve long-term success by staying the course during market volatility.

4. Financial Confidence

Confidence in your investment decisions fosters a sense of financial security and empowerment.

Conclusion

Investing is not just a numbers game; it's a deeply emotional journey. By acknowledging the impact of emotions on your investment decisions, cultivating self-awareness, and implementing strategies to manage emotional biases, you can become a more emotionally intelligent investor.

Remember that emotional intelligence in investing is a skill that can be honed over time, and it can significantly enhance your ability to make sound financial decisions while navigating the complex and ever-changing world of investments.

In the chapters ahead, we will continue to explore the psychology of wealth and provide guidance on achieving financial success while nurturing your mental, emotional, and social well-being, including the art of emotionally intelligent investing in your financial journey.

Chapter 86

Wealth and Sustainable Living

Where we embark on an inspiring journey into the intersection of wealth and sustainable living. Wealth isn't just about accumulating financial assets; it's also about making choices that benefit not only your financial well-being but also the health of our planet and the well-being of future generations. In this chapter, we'll explore the importance of sustainable living, the financial benefits it can offer, and practical strategies for integrating sustainability into your wealth-building journey.

The Significance of Sustainable Living

1. Environmental Stewardship

Sustainable living is an expression of responsible environmental stewardship, helping to protect our planet's resources.

2. Long-Term Prosperity

Sustainability is closely tied to long-term prosperity, as it ensures that resources are available for future generations.

3. Financial Resilience

Sustainable practices can lead to financial resilience by reducing waste, lowering expenses, and creating more efficient systems.

4. Ethical Wealth

Many individuals find deep satisfaction in aligning their wealth-building efforts with their ethical and environmental values.

Practical Strategies for Sustainable Wealth

1. Sustainable Investments

Consider investing in companies and funds that prioritize environmental and social responsibility.

2. Energy Efficiency

Make your home and lifestyle more energy-efficient to reduce utility costs and lower your carbon footprint.

3. Sustainable Transportation

Opt for eco-friendly transportation options, such as electric vehicles or public transit, to save money on fuel and reduce emissions.

4. Minimalism and Conscious Consumption

Embrace a minimalist approach to consumption, focusing on quality over quantity and reducing unnecessary expenses.

The Financial Benefits of Sustainable Living

1. Lower Expenses

Sustainable living often leads to reduced expenses, as you consume less and make more efficient use of resources.

2. Investment Opportunities

Sustainable investments can provide attractive returns while aligning with your values.

3. Tax Incentives

Many governments offer tax incentives and rebates for sustainable practices, further enhancing your financial well-being.

4. Reduced Risk

By diversifying your wealth-building efforts into sustainable ventures, you may reduce exposure to industries vulnerable to environmental risks.

The Rewards of Sustainable Wealth

1. Financial Security

Sustainable living can contribute to financial security by reducing expenses and building wealth through eco-conscious choices.

2. Environmental Impact

You can make a positive impact on the environment, leaving a healthier planet for future generations.

3. Ethical Satisfaction

Achieve a sense of ethical satisfaction by aligning your wealth-building efforts with your values and contributing to positive change.

4. Holistic Well-being

Sustainable wealth integrates financial well-being with environmental and social well-being, fostering a more balanced and fulfilling life.

Conclusion

Wealth and sustainable living are not mutually exclusive; in fact, they complement each other in powerful ways. By recognizing the significance of sustainable living, embracing eco-conscious choices, and integrating sustainability into your financial planning, you can build wealth while leaving a positive legacy for future generations. Remember that wealth is not solely measured by financial assets; it also encompasses the positive impact you make on the world and the well-being of all living beings.

In the chapters ahead, we will continue to explore the psychology of wealth and provide guidance on achieving financial success while nurturing your mental, emotional, and social well-being, including the invaluable role of sustainable living in your financial journey.

Chapter 87

Money and Financial Literacy

Where we embark on an enlightening journey into the world of money and financial literacy. Financial literacy is not just a skill; it's a powerful tool that empowers you to make informed decisions about your finances and secure your financial future. In this chapter, we'll explore the significance of financial literacy, the benefits it offers, and practical strategies for improving your financial knowledge.

The Importance of Financial Literacy

1. Empowerment

Financial literacy empowers you to take control of your financial life, reducing stress and anxiety related to money.

2. Informed Decision-making

It equips you with the knowledge to make informed decisions about budgeting, investing, and debt management.

3. Goal Achievement

Financial literacy helps you turn your financial goals and dreams into achievable realities.

4. Financial Resilience

Being financially literate enhances your ability to navigate economic challenges and setbacks.

The Benefits of Financial Literacy

1. Improved Money Management

Financial literacy enables you to create and stick to a budget, ensuring that you live within your means.

2. Investment Confidence

With financial knowledge, you can confidently make investment decisions that align with your goals and risk tolerance.

3. Debt Management

You'll be better equipped to manage and reduce debt, avoiding high-interest pitfalls.

4. Retirement Planning

Financial literacy is essential for planning a secure and comfortable retirement.

Strategies for Enhancing Financial Literacy

1. Education

Invest in your financial education by reading books, attending seminars, or taking online courses.

2. Budgeting and Tracking

Create a budget and regularly track your income and expenses to understand your financial habits.

3. Seek Expert Advice

Consult with financial advisors or mentors for personalized guidance and advice.

4. Practical Experience

Put your financial knowledge into practice by managing your investments or making financial decisions.

The Rewards of Financial Literacy

1. Financial Independence

Financial literacy can lead to greater financial independence, giving you the confidence to make decisions that align with your goals.

2. Reduced Stress

It reduces financial stress by providing the tools and knowledge to manage money effectively.

3. Goal Attainment

With financial literacy, you're more likely to achieve your financial goals, whether they involve saving for a home, starting a business, or traveling the world.

4. Financial Legacy

You can pass on your financial knowledge and legacy to future generations, setting them up for financial success.

Conclusion

Financial literacy is a valuable asset that can transform your financial journey and shape your future. By recognizing the importance of financial literacy, investing in your financial education, and applying your knowledge to your financial decisions, you can achieve financial independence, reduce stress, and work towards your financial goals with confidence.

Remember that financial literacy is a lifelong journey, and every step you take brings you closer to financial mastery and well-being. In the chapters ahead, we will continue to explore the psychology of wealth and provide guidance on achieving financial success while nurturing your mental, emotional, and social well-being, including the pivotal role of financial literacy in your financial journey.

Chapter 88

The Psychology of Philanthropic Foundations

Where we delve into the intriguing realm of philanthropic foundations, exploring not only the impact they have on society but also the psychology behind their creation and operation. Philanthropy is a powerful force for positive change, and understanding its psychological underpinnings can help individuals and organizations make a more significant difference in the world. In this chapter, we'll explore the motivations behind philanthropy, the strategies philanthropic foundations employ, and the profound impact they can have on shaping a better future.

The Motivations Behind Philanthropy

1. Altruism and Compassion

Many philanthropists are driven by a deep sense of compassion and a desire to make the world a better place.

2. Legacy and Impact

Creating a lasting legacy and leaving a positive impact on society motivate philanthropists to give generously.

3. Personal Fulfillment

Philanthropy often brings a sense of personal fulfillment and purpose to those who engage in it.

4. Social Responsibility

Recognizing a responsibility to address societal issues drives individuals and organizations to contribute to philanthropic causes.

Strategies Employed by Philanthropic Foundations

1. Mission and Focus

Foundations define their mission and focus areas to direct their resources toward specific issues or causes.

2. Grantmaking

Grantmaking is a common strategy, where foundations provide financial support to nonprofits and initiatives aligned with their mission.

3. Collaboration

Foundations often collaborate with other organizations and leverage their expertise to maximize impact.

4. Research and Evaluation

Investing in research and evaluation helps foundations measure the effectiveness of their efforts and make data-driven decisions.

The Impact of Philanthropic Foundations

1. Social Change

Philanthropic foundations play a pivotal role in driving social change and addressing pressing issues, from education and healthcare to environmental conservation.

2. Innovation

They foster innovation by supporting groundbreaking research, innovative solutions, and new approaches to longstanding problems.

3. Community Building

Foundations contribute to the building and strengthening of communities by promoting social cohesion and addressing local needs.

4. Global Reach

Many foundations operate on a global scale, making a positive impact on a worldwide scale.

The Rewards of Philanthropy

1. Fulfillment and Joy

Philanthropists often experience a deep sense of fulfillment and joy from knowing they are making a meaningful difference.

2. Legacy and Recognition

Philanthropy allows individuals and organizations to create a lasting legacy and gain recognition for their positive contributions.

3. Personal Growth

Engaging in philanthropy can lead to personal growth, increased empathy, and a broader perspective on societal issues.

4. Social and Environmental Betterment

The ultimate reward of philanthropy is the positive transformation of society and the environment.

Conclusion

Philanthropic foundations are a driving force for positive change, and the psychology behind their existence is rooted in the human desire to make a difference and leave a legacy of compassion and impact.

By understanding the motivations, strategies, and profound impact of philanthropy, we can inspire others to join in the effort to create a better world. Whether you are an aspiring philanthropist or simply interested in the transformative power of giving, this chapter provides insight into the psychology of philanthropic foundations and their role in shaping a brighter future for all. In the chapters ahead, we will continue to explore the psychology of wealth and provide guidance on achieving financial success while nurturing your mental, emotional, and social well-being, including the transformative potential of philanthropy in your financial journey.

Chapter 89

Wealth and Emotional Intelligence in Business

The dynamic interplay between wealth and emotional intelligence in the world of business. Success in the business realm is not solely dependent on financial acumen; Emotional intelligence plays a pivotal role in fostering strong leadership, building meaningful relationships, and achieving sustainable wealth. In this chapter, we'll explore the significance of emotional intelligence in business, its impact on financial outcomes, and practical strategies for enhancing emotional intelligence to drive business success.

The Significance of Emotional Intelligence in Business

1. Leadership Effectiveness

Emotionally intelligent leaders inspire and motivate their teams, driving innovation and productivity.

2. Relationship Building

Strong interpersonal skills and empathy enable successful networking and collaboration in the business world.

3. Decision making

Emotional intelligence aids in making informed, rational decisions and managing risk effectively.

4. Adaptability

Emotionally intelligent individuals and businesses are better equipped to adapt to change and navigate challenges.

The Impact of Emotional Intelligence on Financial Outcomes

1. Team Performance

Emotionally intelligent leaders foster high-performing teams, which can translate into increased profitability.

2. Client and Customer Relations

Strong client and customer relationships based on trust and empathy often lead to increased sales and loyalty.

3. Negotiation and Conflict Resolution

Emotional intelligence enhances negotiation skills and facilitates successful conflict resolution, preserving business relationships.

4. Employee retention

Businesses that prioritize emotional intelligence often experience higher employee retention rates, reducing recruitment and training costs.

Strategies for Enhancing Emotional Intelligence in Business

1. Self-awareness

Recognize your own emotions and triggers to better understand their impact on your decisions and interactions.

2. Empathy

Develop empathy by actively listening and seeking to understand the perspectives and feelings of others.

3. Communication Skills

Improve communication skills, including verbal and non-verbal cues, to convey messages effectively.

4. Conflict Resolution

Learn effective conflict resolution techniques to address issues promptly and constructively.

The Rewards of Emotional Intelligence in Business

1. Leadership Excellence

Emotionally intelligent leaders inspire and motivate their teams, driving business success and personal growth.

2. Strong Relationships

Building strong relationships with clients, customers, and colleagues fosters trust and long-term business success.

3. Wise decision makin

Emotional intelligence aids in making informed and rational business decisions, reducing risks and maximizing opportunities.

4. Resilience

Emotionally intelligent individuals and businesses are more resilient and adaptable in the face of challenges.

Conclusion

Emotional intelligence is a powerful asset in the world of business, and its impact on financial success cannot be overstated. By recognizing the significance of emotional intelligence, nurturing self-awareness, empathy, and effective communication, individuals and businesses can create an environment conducive to growth, innovation, and lasting wealth.

Whether you are an entrepreneur, a business leader, or simply interested in the role of emotional intelligence in business, this chapter sheds light on the essential connection between wealth and emotional intelligence in the corporate world.

In the chapters ahead, we will continue to explore the psychology of wealth and provide guidance on achieving financial success while nurturing your mental, emotional, and social well-being, including the pivotal role of emotional intelligence in the business landscape.

Chapter 90

Money and Philanthropic Impact

We embark on a journey to explore the profound connection between money and philanthropic impact. Money has the power to effect positive change in the world, and philanthropy provides a meaningful avenue to make a difference in the lives of individuals, communities, and causes you care deeply about. In this chapter, we'll delve into the significance of philanthropic impact, the strategies for maximizing the effectiveness of your giving, and the transformative rewards it brings to both the giver and the recipients.

The Significance of Philanthropic Impact

1 Transforming Lives

Philanthropy has the potential to transform the lives of those in need, providing opportunities and support where it's most needed.

2 Addressing Social Challenges

Philanthropic impact plays a vital role in addressing complex social challenges, from poverty and healthcare to education and environmental conservation.

3 Fostering Positive Change

By supporting charitable causes, you contribute to the betterment of society and inspire others to join in creating a brighter future.

4 Personal Fulfillment

Philanthropic giving often brings a deep sense of personal fulfillment, purpose, and joy.

Strategies for Maximizing Philanthropic Impact

1 Define Your Mission

Clarify your philanthropic mission and identify the causes or issues that resonate with your values and passions.

2 Strategic Giving

Strategically allocate your resources to maximize the impact of your philanthropy, targeting areas where your support can make a significant difference.

3 Collaborate and Partner

Collaborate with other philanthropists, organizations, and experts to amplify your impact and leverage collective resources.

4 Measure and Evaluate

Regularly assess the effectiveness of your philanthropic efforts through metrics, impact assessments, and feedback from beneficiaries.

The Rewards of Philanthropic Impact

1 Making a Difference

Philanthropic impact allows you to make a tangible, positive difference in the lives of others and in the world.

2 Legacy and Recognition

Generous giving can create a lasting legacy and recognition for your contributions to society.

3 Personal Growth

Engaging in philanthropy fosters personal growth, increased empathy, and a deeper understanding of social issues.

4 Inspiring Change

Your philanthropic actions inspire others to get involved and contribute to the causes they are passionate about.

Conclusion

Money and philanthropic impact are intrinsically linked, offering an extraordinary opportunity to effect positive change in the world while experiencing personal growth and fulfillment. By recognizing the significance of philanthropic impact, defining your mission, and employing strategic giving practices, you can leave a lasting legacy of compassion and contribute to a brighter future for all.

Whether you are a seasoned philanthropist or someone looking to make their first philanthropic contribution, this chapter sheds light on the incredible potential of money to create meaningful, transformative impact. In the chapters ahead, we will continue to explore the psychology of wealth and provide guidance on achieving financial success while nurturing your mental, emotional, and social well-being.

Chapter 91

Wealth and Success Mindset

Where we delve into the fascinating connection between wealth and a success mindset. Your mindset is a powerful tool that can shape your financial journey, determine your actions, and ultimately lead you toward wealth and prosperity. In this chapter, we'll explore the significance of a success mindset, the impact it has on wealth-building, and practical strategies for cultivating and nurturing this mindset.

The Significance of a Success Mindset

1. Vision and Purpose

A success mindset provides you with a clear vision and purpose, guiding your financial goals and aspirations.

2. Resilience

It fosters resilience in the face of setbacks and challenges, helping you persevere on your wealth-building journey.

3. Confidence

A success mindset boosts your self-confidence and belief in your ability to achieve financial success.

4. Abundance Mentality

It cultivates an abundance mentality, allowing you to see opportunities and possibilities where others may see limitations.

The Impact of a Success Mindset on Wealth Building

1. Goal Achievement

Individuals with a success mindset are more likely to set and achieve ambitious financial goals.

2. Risk taking

They are more willing to take calculated risks, which can lead to greater financial rewards.

3. Adaptability

A success mindset promotes adaptability, helping you navigate changing financial landscapes.

4. Wealth Attraction

A positive and determined mindset can attract wealth by opening doors to new opportunities and connections.

Strategies for Cultivating a Success Mindset

1. Set Clear Goals

Define your financial goals with precision and create a plan to achieve them.

2. Positive Self Talk

Practice positive self-talk and replace self-limiting beliefs with empowering affirmations.

3. Continuous Learning

Invest in your education and personal development to stay informed and adaptive in your financial endeavors.

4. Resilience Building

Develop resilience by viewing setbacks as learning experiences and opportunities for growth.

The Rewards of a Success Mindset

1. Achievement

A success mindset leads to tangible achievements, bringing your financial goals within reach.

2. Confidence and Belief

It boosts your confidence and belief in your ability to overcome challenges and prosper.

3. Wealth Building

A success mindset accelerates your wealth-building journey by attracting opportunities and resources.

4. Personal Growth

Engaging in the pursuit of a success mindset fosters personal growth and a sense of fulfillment.

Conclusion

A success mindset is a powerful force that can propel you toward wealth and prosperity by shaping your thoughts, actions, and beliefs. By recognizing the significance of a success mindset, setting clear goals, practicing positive self-talk, and continually nurturing your mindset, you can achieve financial success while experiencing personal growth and fulfillment.

Whether you are an aspiring entrepreneur, a seasoned investor, or someone simply interested in the connection between mindset and wealth, this chapter sheds light on the transformative potential of adopting a success mindset in your financial journey.

In the chapters ahead, we will continue to explore the psychology of wealth and provide guidance on achieving financial success while nurturing your mental, emotional, and social well-being, including the invaluable role of a success mindset in your financial journey.

Chapter 92

The Psychological Benefits of a Financial Safety Net

We delve into the profound psychological benefits of having a financial safety net. A financial safety net is like a cushion that provides peace of mind and security in an unpredictable world. In this chapter, we'll explore the significance of having a financial safety net, the impact it has on your mental and emotional well-being, and practical strategies for building and maintaining one.

The Significance of a Financial Safety Net

1 Peace of Mind

A financial safety net offers peace of mind, reducing stress and anxiety related to unexpected expenses or financial emergencies.

2 Sense of Security

It provides a sense of security and stability, allowing you to navigate life's challenges with confidence.

3 Freedom to Pursue Goals

Having a safety net enables you to pursue your goals and aspirations without the constant worry of financial setbacks.

4 Reduced Fear of the Unknown

A safety net reduces the fear of the unknown, giving you the courage to take calculated risks and embrace change.

The Impact of a Financial Safety Net on Mental and Emotional Well-being

1 Reduced Stress

Knowing you have a financial cushion can significantly reduce stress levels, promoting overall mental health.

2 Improved Decision-Making

With less financial pressure, you can make better decisions and focus on long-term goals.

3 Enhanced Resilience

A safety net builds emotional resilience, helping you bounce back from adversity and setbacks.

4 Better Relationships

Financial stability fosters healthier relationships by reducing conflict and stress within families and partnerships.

Strategies for Building and Maintaining a Financial Safety Net

1 Emergency Fund

Create an emergency fund with three to six months' worth of living expenses to cover unexpected costs.

2 Insurance Coverage

Invest in appropriate insurance coverage, such as health, life, and disability insurance, to protect against major financial risks.

3 Budgeting and Saving

Practice budgeting and regular saving to ensure your safety net remains intact and continues to grow.

4 Diversify Investments

Diversify your investments to reduce risk and provide additional financial security.

The Rewards of a Financial Safety Net

1 Peace of Mind

A financial safety net offers the invaluable gift of peace of mind, allowing you to sleep soundly at night.

2 Confidence

It boosts your confidence in handling financial challenges and pursuing your dreams.

3 Improved Mental Health

Reduced financial stress contributes to improved mental health and overall well-being.

4 Better Quality of Life

With a safety net in place, you can enjoy a higher quality of life, free from constant financial worry.

Conclusion

A financial safety net isn't just about dollars and cents; it's about your peace of mind, security, and emotional well-being. By recognizing the significance of having a financial safety net, taking proactive steps to build and maintain one, and experiencing the profound psychological benefits it brings, you can navigate life's uncertainties with confidence and embrace the future with optimism.

Whether you are just beginning to build your safety net or have already established one, this chapter sheds light on the transformative power of financial security in your life journey.

In the chapters ahead, we will continue to explore the psychology of wealth and provide guidance on achieving financial success while nurturing your mental, emotional, and social well-being.

Chapter 93
Money and the Art of Negotiating Salary

We explore the art of negotiating your salary—a skill that can significantly impact your financial well-being and career satisfaction. Negotiating your salary isn't just about money; it's about recognizing your worth, advocating for yourself, and setting the stage for financial success. In this chapter, we'll delve into the significance of salary negotiation, strategies for mastering this art, and how it can contribute to your financial growth and overall career fulfillment.

The Significance of Salary Negotiation

1 Fair Compensation

Negotiating your salary ensures that you receive fair and equitable compensation for your skills, experience, and contributions.

2 Financial Growth

A successful negotiation can set the stage for future earnings, leading to significant financial growth over your career.

3 Self-Advocacy

Salary negotiation is an opportunity to advocate for yourself and your financial well-being, building confidence in your worth.

4 Career Satisfaction

Negotiating a competitive salary contributes to career satisfaction and a sense of value within your organization.

The Impact of Salary Negotiation on Financial Growth

1 Increased Earnings

Successful negotiations can lead to higher initial salaries and subsequent raises, compounding your overall earnings.

2 Retirement Savings

Higher earnings enable you to save more for retirement, securing your financial future.

3 Investment Opportunities

Additional income from successful negotiations can be directed towards investments, accelerating wealth accumulation.

4 Debt Reduction

Negotiating a higher salary can help you pay off debt more quickly, reducing financial stress.

Strategies for Mastering the Art of Salary Negotiation

1 Research

Thoroughly research industry salary standards and the specific compensation practices of your potential employer.

2 Prepare

Prepare a compelling case that highlights your skills, accomplishments, and the value you bring to the organization.

3 Practice

Practice your negotiation skills with a trusted friend or mentor to build confidence and refine your approach.

4 Be Flexible

Be open to negotiation and consider the entire compensation package, including benefits and bonuses.

The Rewards of Successful Salary Negotiation

1 Financial Growth

Negotiating a higher salary directly contributes to your financial growth and wealth-building potential.

2 Confidence

Successful negotiations boost your confidence in advocating for your financial interests.

3 Career Satisfaction

Receiving fair compensation enhances career satisfaction and job engagement.

4 Improved Financial Well-being

Higher earnings from successful negotiations positively impact your overall financial well-being.

Conclusion

The art of negotiating your salary is a valuable skill that can shape your financial future and career satisfaction. By recognizing the significance of salary negotiation, preparing effectively, practicing your negotiation skills, and reaping the rewards of financial growth and career satisfaction, you can set a solid foundation for your financial success.

Whether you are preparing for your first salary negotiation or seeking to enhance your negotiation skills, this chapter sheds light on the transformative power of advocating for your worth in your financial journey.

In the chapters ahead, we will continue to explore the psychology of wealth and provide guidance on achieving financial success while nurturing your mental, emotional, and social well-being.

Chapter 94

Wealth and Financial Legacy

We delve into the profound significance of wealth and financial legacy—a legacy that extends far beyond your lifetime and leaves a lasting impact on future generations. Your financial legacy is not merely a sum of money; it encompasses the values, principles, and wisdom you pass down to your loved ones and the world. In this chapter, we'll explore the importance of creating a meaningful financial legacy, the strategies for building and preserving it, and the transformative rewards it brings to both you and your heirs.

The Significance of a Financial Legacy

1 Perpetuating Values

A financial legacy enables you to perpetuate your core values, beliefs, and principles through generations.

2 Impact on Future Generations

It has the power to shape the lives and opportunities of your descendants, providing them with a foundation for success.

3 Philanthropic Giving

A financial legacy allows you to support charitable causes and make a lasting impact on society.

4 Personal Fulfillment

Creating a financial legacy often brings a deep sense of personal fulfillment, knowing that your wealth serves a meaningful purpose.

The Impact of a Financial Legacy on Future Generations

1 Financial Security

A well-structured legacy can provide financial security and opportunities for your heirs, promoting their well-being.

2 Education and Advancement

It can fund education and personal development, empowering your descendants to achieve their aspirations.

3 Philanthropic Values

A financial legacy can instill philanthropic values, encouraging your heirs to give back to the community.

4 Family Unity

Passing down a financial legacy can strengthen family bonds and promote unity through shared goals.

Strategies for Building and Preserving a Financial Legacy

1 Estate Planning

Engage in comprehensive estate planning to ensure that your assets are distributed according to your wishes.

2 Educate and Communicate

Educate your heirs about financial responsibility and the values you wish to instill in them. Open and clear communication is key.

3 Philanthropic Giving

Consider philanthropic giving as a way to leave a positive impact on society and involve your heirs in charitable endeavors.

4 Wealth Preservation

Implement wealth preservation strategies, such as trusts and investments, to safeguard your legacy.

The Rewards of a Financial Legacy

1 Lasting Impact

A financial legacy leaves a lasting impact on the lives of your descendants and the causes you care about.

2 Family Unity

It promotes family unity and shared values, fostering strong bonds among generations.

3 Personal Fulfillment

Creating a financial legacy often brings a profound sense of personal fulfillment and purpose.

4 Legacy of Giving

Your legacy can inspire future generations to continue the tradition of giving and making a positive impact.

Conclusion

A financial legacy is a testament to your values, wisdom, and the love you have for your family and community. By recognizing the significance of a financial legacy, implementing sound estate planning, educating and communicating with your heirs, and experiencing the transformative rewards it brings, you can leave a lasting legacy that transcends generations and contributes to a brighter future.

Whether you are at the beginning of your wealth-building journey or are already considering your legacy, this chapter sheds light on the profound impact of creating a financial legacy in your life's journey. In the chapters ahead, we will continue to explore the psychology of wealth and provide guidance on achieving financial success while nurturing your mental, emotional, and social well-being.

Chapter 95

The Role of Empathy in Wealth Psychology

We dive into the captivating realm of empathy and its profound role in wealth psychology. While wealth often conjures up images of financial abundance, it's equally essential to recognize the wealth of empathy quality that enriches our lives, relationships, and financial well-being. In this chapter, we'll explore the significance of empathy, its impact on financial decisions, strategies for nurturing empathy in your financial journey, and the transformative rewards it brings to both you and your community.

The Significance of Empathy

1 Connection with Others

Empathy fosters genuine connections with others, creating a sense of unity and understanding.

2 Emotional Intelligence

It enhances emotional intelligence, allowing you to navigate complex social and financial situations with grace.

3 Compassionate Decision-Making

Empathy guides compassionate decision-making, enabling you to consider the well-being of others in your financial choices.

4 Community Building

Empathy plays a crucial role in building supportive and thriving communities.

The Impact of Empathy on Financial Decisions

1 Philanthropic Giving

Empathy often drives philanthropic giving, as it compels you to support causes that align with your values.

2 Fair Business Practices

In business, empathy can lead to fair and ethical practices, promoting trust and long-term success.

3 Wealth Sharin

Empathy may encourage wealth sharing and collaborative financial strategies, benefiting both individuals and communities.

4 Relationship Building

Empathy enhances relationships, fostering trust and cooperation in financial partnerships.

Strategies for Nurturing Empathy in Your Financial Journey

1 Active Listening

Practice active listening to truly understand the perspectives and needs of others in financial discussions.

2 Perspective-Taking

Put yourself in others' shoes to gain insight into their financial challenges and motivations.

3 Volunteering and Giving

Engage in volunteering and charitable giving to directly experience the impact of empathy on your financial decisions.

4 Cultivate Gratitude

Cultivate gratitude for your financial resources, which can inspire empathy for those facing financial hardships.

The Rewards of Empathy

1 Fulfilling Relationships

Empathy enriches your relationships, creating deep connections with others.

2 Compassionate Financial Decisions

It guides compassionate financial decisions that benefit both individuals and society.

3 Personal Growth

Practicing empathy fosters personal growth, increasing your emotional intelligence and understanding of human dynamics.

4 Stronger Communities

Empathy contributes to the creation of stronger, more supportive communities.

Conclusion

Empathy is a wealth of the heart treasure that enriches our financial lives and extends its influence to the greater good of humanity. By recognizing the significance of empathy, practicing active listening and perspective-taking, and experiencing the transformative rewards it brings, you can infuse your financial journey with compassion and understanding.

Whether you are seeking to enhance your empathetic abilities or are already guided by empathy in your financial decisions, this chapter sheds light on the profound role of empathy in wealth psychology and its enduring impact on your financial well-being.

In the chapters ahead, we will continue to explore the psychology of wealth and provide guidance on achieving financial success while nurturing your mental, emotional, and social well-being, including the pivotal role of empathy in your financial strategy.

Chapter 96

Money and Personal Growth

We explore the intricate relationship between money and personal growth—an essential journey that goes beyond financial success to encompass your overall well-being and development. Money, when viewed as a tool for personal growth, can open doors to self-discovery, empowerment, and fulfillment. In this chapter, we'll delve into the significance of money in personal growth, the ways it can catalyze your self-development, practical strategies for aligning your financial goals with personal growth, and the enriching rewards it brings to your life.

The Significance of Money in Personal Growth

1. Financial Freedom

Money provides the freedom to pursue personal growth opportunities without the constraints of financial stress.

2. Self discovery

Financial resources can facilitate self-discovery by allowing you to explore new interests, hobbies, and experiences.

3. Education and Development

Money enables you to invest in education, skill development, and personal growth resources.

4. empowerment

Financial independence empowers you to make choices aligned with your personal values and aspirations.

Ways Money Can Catalyze Personal Growth

1. Education and Learning

Investing in education and lifelong learning expands your knowledge and personal growth potential.

2. Pursuing Passions

Money can fund the pursuit of passions and interests that bring fulfillment and personal growth.

3. Travel and Exploration

Financial resources facilitate travel and exploration, broadening your perspective and fostering personal growth.

4. Health and Well-being

Money can be used to invest in your health and well-being, supporting physical and emotional growth.

Strategies for Aligning Money and Personal Growth

1. Set Personal Growth Goals

Define personal growth goals and incorporate them into your financial planning.

2. Budget for Self-Development

Allocate a portion of your budget to activities and resources that promote personal growth.

3. Invest Wisely

Invest your resources in assets, experiences, and opportunities that contribute to personal development.

4. Seek Guidance

Consider seeking financial advice and guidance to align your financial goals with personal growth.

The Rewards of Embracing Money for Personal Growth

1. Self discovery

The journey of using money for personal growth leads to greater self-discovery and self-awareness.

2. Fulfillment

Investing in personal growth brings a profound sense of fulfillment and purpose to your life.

3. empowerment

Financial independence empowers you to take control of your life and shape your own destiny.

4. Balanced Well-being

Aligning money with personal growth fosters a balanced and enriched overall well-being.

Conclusion

Money can be a catalyst for personal growth, allowing you to explore your potential, discover your passions, and embark on a transformative journey of self-improvement.

By recognizing the significance of money in personal growth, setting clear personal growth goals, budgeting for self-development, and experiencing the enriching rewards it brings to your life, you can harness the power of financial resources to not only achieve monetary success but also foster personal growth and fulfillment.

Whether you are just beginning your personal growth journey or seeking to enhance your financial strategy to support it, this chapter sheds light on the profound connection between money and personal growth in your life's journey.

In the chapters ahead, we will continue to explore the psychology of wealth and provide guidance on achieving financial success while nurturing your mental, emotional, and social well-being, including the role of money in fostering personal growth.

Chapter 97

Conclusion

Mastering Wealth Psychology

Congratulations on embarking on this enlightening journey through the world of wealth psychology! As we reach the conclusion of this comprehensive exploration, it's time to reflect on the transformative insights and wisdom you've gained to master the intricate art of wealth psychology. This chapter serves as both a recap of your journey and a guidepost for your continued pursuit of financial success, well-being, and fulfillment.

Reflecting on Your Wealth Psychology Journey

1. Understanding Your Money Beliefs

You began your journey by exploring your deeply rooted money beliefs, uncovering how they shape your financial decisions, and recognizing the power of mindset in wealth creation.

2. Overcoming Financial Limitations

You learned how to overcome financial limitations, break free from self-imposed constraints, and embrace a growth-oriented mindset that empowers you to achieve your financial goals.

3. Setting and Achieving Financial Goals

You delved into the psychology of setting and achieving financial goals, discovering how clarity, focus, and determination are key ingredients in the recipe for financial success.

4. Navigating Wealth and Happiness

You explore the intricate relationship between wealth and happiness, realizing that true wealth goes beyond money and encompasses the richness of well-being, purpose, and contentment.

5. Building Wealth Through Financial Planning

You examined the role of financial planning in psychological well-being, recognizing the importance of prudent financial management in creating a secure and fulfilling future.

6. Cultivating Emotional Intelligence for Wealth

You explored the connection between wealth and emotional intelligence, understanding how emotional awareness and regulation are essential for making sound financial decisions.

7. Your Relationship with Money

You uncovered the intricacies of your relationship with money, gaining insights into how it impacts your self-worth, self-esteem, and overall financial well-being.

8th. Coping with Financial Stress

You learned effective strategies for managing financial stress, equipping yourself with tools to navigate financial challenges with resilience and composure.

9. The Power of Wealth Visualization

You harnessed the power of wealth visualization techniques, using the imagination to shape your financial future and manifest your financial goals.

10. Wealth and Generosity

You explored the profound connection between wealth and generosity, realizing that giving not only benefits others but also enriches your own life.

11. The Role of Patience in Wealth Building

You recognized the importance of patience in wealth building, understanding that long-term financial success often requires endurance and perseverance.

12. Money and work-life balance

You explore the delicate balance between money and work-life balance, discovering the value of prioritizing well-being and relationships alongside financial goals.

13. Wealth and Risk Taking

You delved into the psychology of risk-taking, learning how to make informed financial decisions that align with your risk tolerance and goals.

14. The Psychology of Entrepreneurship

You explored the mindset of entrepreneurship, uncovering the traits and attitudes that can lead to business success and financial fulfillment.

15. Wealth and Education

You recognized the importance of education in wealth acquisition, understanding how learning and knowledge can open doors to financial growth.

16. The Emotional Cost of Impulse Buying

You explored the emotional impact of impulse buying, gaining insights into how mindful spending contributes to financial well-being.

17. Wealth and Retirement Planning

You learned the importance of retirement planning, ensuring a financially secure and fulfilling retirement that aligns with your long-term goals.

18. Overcoming Scarcity Mindset

You tackled the scarcity mindset, shifting your perspective toward abundance and fostering a positive relationship with money.

19. Money and Social Comparison

You explored the psychology of social comparison, understanding how it can impact your financial decisions and well-being.

20. The Psychology of Giving Back

You uncovered the psychology of philanthropy, discovering the personal and societal benefits of giving to others.

21. Financial Self Care

You learned the importance of financial self-care, recognizing that taking care of your financial well-being is an act of self-love and empowerment.

22. The Connection Between Mindfulness and Wealth

You embraced mindfulness as a tool for managing your finances and enhancing your overall psychology wealth.

23. The Impact of Social Media on Financial Well-being

You examined the influence of social media on

financial well-being, learning how to navigate the digital world while maintaining financial balance.

24. Wealth and Identity

You explored the connection between wealth and identity, recognizing that true wealth is about aligning your financial choices with your authentic self.

25. Coping with Financial Loss

You learned strategies for coping with financial loss, building resilience in the face of setbacks, and maintaining a positive financial outlook.

26. The Psychology of Homeownership

You delved into the psychology of homeownership, understanding the emotional and financial aspects of owning a home.

27. Wealth and Philanthropy

You explore the intersection of wealth and philanthropy, recognizing the potential for meaningful impact through charitable giving.

28. Financial Resilience

You discovered the importance of financial resilience, equipping yourself with the skills to bounce back from financial challenges and setbacks.

29. Wealth and Personal Growth

You explore the enriching connection between money and personal growth, realizing that financial resources can catalyze self-discovery and empowerment.

30. Navigating Economic Downturns

You learned how to navigate economic downturns with resilience and adaptability, ensuring your financial well-being in uncertain times.

31. Money and the Pursuit of Passion

You embraced the pursuit of passion as a means of achieving financial fulfillment and personal growth.

32. Wealth and Family Dynamics

You explore the dynamics of wealth within families, recognizing the importance of open communication and shared values.

33. The Psychology of Luxury

Afterword

As we conclude this exploration of wealth psychology, remember that true wealth is not just what you have, but who you become. May your financial journey be one of growth, generosity, and grace.

Author's Note

This book is born from my journey from Eritrea to Germany—a journey not just of geography, but of mindset. It is my hope that these lessons in wealth psychology help you build a life of freedom, purpose, and abundance.

www.ingramcontent.com/pod-product-compliance
Lightning Source LLC
LaVergne TN
LVHW052032200926
848481LV00005B/1656